This is a book about fruit, but not apples and oranges.
The other fruit.

This is a book about sex, but not just sex.
Sex is never alone.

This is a book about love and truth, about you and I and him and her. It's about finding something beautiful, delightful, joyful, precious and good and taking big bites of it. It's about taking the dirty clothes off of that fruit and seeing it for the naked beauty it is.

Or, at least, can be ...

THE NAKED FRUIT

mango ink publishing
the naked fruit
copyright © 2010 by ryan miller

mango ink publishing

All scripture quotations, unless otherwise indicated, are taken from the HOLY BIBLE, NEW INTERNATIONAL VERSION®. NIV®. Copyright © 1973, 1978, 1984 by International Bible Society. Used by permission of Zondervan. All rights reserved.

Mango Ink Publishing

All Rights Reserved. No part of this book may be reproduced or transmitted in any form or by any means, graphic, electronic, or mechanical, including photocopying, recording, taping, or any information storage retrieval system, without the written permission of the publisher.

ISBN: 978-0615-2773-32

Printed in the United States of America

cover design: Nick Tibbetts
photographer: Ben Fowler
model: Kyle Taylor

THE NAKED FRUIT
HER. HIM. SEX. LOVE. TRUTH.

RYAN MILLER

thenaked**fruit**

intro**move**
01**her and him**
02**knowing**
03**skin with a twist**
04**women**
05**fight**
06**boomerang**
07**love is fruit**
08**mangos**
09**hero**
10**this is where**
11**partners**
12**happily ever after**
13**the soul of the matter**
14**endings**
gratitude**endnotes**

to**beauty**

*Artists understand that they have the power,
through gifts,
innovation and love,
to create a new story,
one that's better than the old one.*

Seth Godin, Linchpin

intro.move.

We need to be moved.

Yesterday, I just found out about another couple: married over fifteen years, three kids, and the husband is having an affair. The kids are shattered right now, trying to collect the pieces because mom and dad are getting a divorce.

It's always amazing to me how something as simple as sex
can be so beautiful
and so destructive.

It's a hurting system, contaminated with lies, coercion, abuse, slavery, and brokenness . . . from sex slaves to sex addicts and everything in-between.

Some of us simply aren't aware.
Maybe this book can move you.

Some of us are not concerned.
Maybe this book can move you.

Some of us don't know what to do.
Maybe this book can move you.

We're all involved, whether we know it or not.
We need to be moved into a better story.

If you read this book and are moved, feel free to pass it along, and tell others to do the same. There are also free digital versions at the website www.thenakedfruit.com.

Maybe this book can move us all. Just a little.

Away from the destructive stories
and back to the beautiful stories.

Craftiness must have clothes but truth loves to go naked.

English Proverb

one. her and him.

Beautiful.
Delightful.
Joyful.
Precious.
Good.

She was fourteen when she was kidnapped. She was taken to a mountain cabin where she was tied up with a cable. She was raped repeatedly, every day, for nine months.[1] She testified in court today.

Beautiful.
Delightful.
Joyful.
Precious.
Good.

The governor of California was just asked by a member of the British government to shut down a website.[2] The website consists of thousands of "field reports" of prostitutes. Here are a few examples of those reports …

> Her breasts weren't as big as her profile said.
> We chatted for a while first to get comfortable.
> She loves oral sex.
> In the end … would you recommend her or not?[3]

Those are two stories that just happened to appear on my news feed today.

Just today.

They appear every day and there are many that are much worse.

Beautiful.
Delightful.
Joyful.

THE NAKED FRUIT

Precious.
Good.

What happened? Where did you go? Were you ever really here?

her
She was beautiful, delightful, joyful, precious … good.

Think about the most beautiful face you have ever seen.
Eyes, skin, hair, cheeks, lips.

Imagine the sexiest body you can.
Legs, stomach, hips, waist, chest.

Some math guys at Cambridge studied women extensively and came up with a perfect ratio of hips to waist size. They say the closer the waist is to 70% of the hips, the sexier the walk.[4] It turns out that Marilyn Monroe's number was 69% and Jessica Alba's is a perfect 70%. In other words, scientists have now determined that Jessica Alba has a really good walk.

I imagine *she* had the walk. I imagine *she* had some other things going for her too. Not just looks.

She pretty much had it all, or at least all that is covered under beautiful, delightful, joyful, precious, and good. Those are all pretty big words.

She was also naked. Sometimes, people use the idea of "being naked" because they think it makes them hip. I once heard an actress say she walks around her house naked all the time. To be honest, I was not that impressed. I imagined my wife and me walking around naked and making our kids' lunches in the morning and, well, it doesn't fit. But it fit with her. She didn't know any better. She wasn't trying to impress anyone. It was natural, real, and beautiful.

It was innocent.

It was … good.

him
If you've heard of her, you've heard of the man who was with her. He was worthy to be her man. We all know a couple or two who just don't

her and him

match. We ask ourselves how she ended up with him or he ended up with her. Not them.

They were both ... good.

In many ways, good means "complete." Remember Jerry Maguire and "you complete me"? They completed each other in every way that they could be completed. And, they were naked. Innocent. Precious.

The spot they lived was pretty good too. It was a beautiful, delightful, joyous place. Probably some lush palm trees. Warm breezes. Moonlit nights. Waterfalls. Natural hot springs. You get the picture.

You want to go to this good spot and be these good people.

We all do. Even if we think we don't, we do.

So, they were good. The spot was good. I don't want to get too weird, but I can't help but imagine the kind of sex these two had. One of my favorite song lyrics is from Elisa and it talks about having her soul rocked. I would bet money they had sex that rocked each others souls.

Beautiful. Delightful. Joyful. Precious. Sex. It was all there.

I don't know if it was perfect. I don't know if I even want it to be perfect. Sometimes I'm not sure I even know what perfect means. But, if you give me enough beautiful, delightful, joyful, precious, and good ... well, I don't think I would care that much whether it was perfect or not.

One day the whole good thing went to Hell.

Not good.

It all started with some words that were not true. Words that aren't true are lies.

Lies are very powerful
                      as long as someone believes them.

It's interesting that a lie is defined as "an intentionally false statement".

If these words, that were not true, turned everything from good to not good than that means someone or something was intending for that to happen.

Who the hell doesn't want beautiful, delightful, joyful, precious, and good?

us
There is something else interesting. The words that were not true were all about fruit. She listened to some words about fruit, looked at some fruit, took a bite of some fruit, and the rest is history.

They went from naked to needing clothes. They went from tropical paradise to pulling weeds. All of that good started to be replaced by things like work, sweat, regret, pain, ugliness, jealousy, loneliness … you get the picture.

At this point, you may have picked up on the story: Adam and Eve. Yeah, that crazy one.

I don't know if the story literally happened. I don't think it did. But, I don't think it matters because I know it's true.

I know it's true because it happens every day.

> Things are good.
>
> There are lies.
>
> Things get really screwed up.

So don't let the crazy parts throw you off. It's just a story about moving from beautiful, delightful, joyful, precious and good to the kind of stuff I read on my Yahoo newsfeed every day.

Things got really screwed up because something other than good entered the picture with the intention of messing up good. If something's intention is messing up good, then I can only assume that something is probably the opposite of good, evil.

I don't know what evil looks like to you. Darth Vader. Rape. The Pope. Maybe you think evil doesn't exist. I think it does.

her and him

Evil is like your grandma's perfume. It permeates and clings. You put on the shirt you wore to Thanksgiving, and you look around to see if your grandma is in your closet with you before you remember hugging her five days ago.

I think of evil like that. It sticks. If the world is a house, the story of Adam and Eve is about evil coming into the house and lighting a nasty-smelling cigarette and blowing toxic smoke all over the place. The nasty smell has clung to our lamp shades, to our couch, to our ceiling, and to our mattress and pillows.

I can smell it on my Yahoo newsfeed today. If you pay attention, or even if you don't, I'm sure you smell it too.

What about the whole fruit thing?

That part of the story has stuck with us too. There are all kinds of things we call forbidden fruits today: mainly things that look tasty, appealing, and good but that end up screwing up our lives later on down the road when we realize we've moved a long way from good. Most of the time those things have something to do with sex or sexuality.

The problem with forbidden things is that we don't like people to tell us that we can or cannot do something. It's built into our nature. So, forbidden fruit really has a bad rap. We are torn up about this forbidden fruit, even though we pretend we aren't.

We agree it stinks in our house but we don't like to be told something smells so we pretend it doesn't and somehow that makes us feel better.

If we really think about Adam and Eve, we start to realize that we're a lot like them. We start to realize their story is a lot like our story.

Adam and Eve are still walking around, but the names have changed to my name and yours. You and I still have those fruits in front of us. There are voices telling us that the fruit shouldn't be forbidden, isn't forbidden, or we should eat it. The fruit is sexual, and we're usually naked when we're about to eat it. We might have our clothes off or we might just be exposed and vulnerable.

Maybe all three.

17

THE NAKED FRUIT

Just like her and just like him. Here we are.

was
It's really easy to focus on the "there was deception" and "things got really screwed up" parts of the story. The negative. The crappy part.

Religion often does that.

We have to remember that this thing started off good.
It *moved* to screwed up and negative.

It was beautiful.
It *moved* to ugly.

It was delightful.
It *moved* somewhere else.

Do we think there is a way to *move* it back there? Back toward good? Or if you believe it never was good, can we get there for the first time?

That story about Adam and Eve has an interesting point that we don't think about that often. Adam and Eve had a tropical, lush, garden honeymoon paradise filled with good fruit. In the midst of that cornucopia of taste, there was one fruit that was a bad one.

One.

Thousands of good fruit and one bad one.

If we have to have the term forbidden fruit, that means that not all fruit is forbidden.

If not all fruit is forbidden, that means that there is some fruit that is really good. In fact, it's recommended fruit. Tasty fruit. Luscious fruit. Sweet fruit.

Beautiful, delightful, joyful, precious, and good fruit.

Why do we always focus on the one bad fruit when there were thousands of good fruits?

Maybe there are some lies today. Maybe the lies are putting all of the attention on the forbidden fruit so that we forget all of the good fruits. That's the intention of the lies. But if we can somehow manage to not listen to the lies, to get the smoke out of our house, we might find something good there, right in front of us.

We might move back toward the "things were really good" part of the story.

Maybe we can understand fruit. Maybe we can understand forbidden. Maybe we can understand luscious. Maybe we can identify the lies. Maybe we can find a way to move away from metal chains, rape, and rating women who are paid to have sex back toward …

Beautiful.

Delightful.

Joyful.

Precious.

Good.

You can get a large audience together for a strip-tease act – that is, to watch a girl undress on the stage. Now suppose you came to a country where you could fill a theatre by simply bringing a covered plate on to the stage and then slowly lifting the cover so as to let every one see, just before the lights went out, that it contained a mutton chop or a bit of bacon, would you not think that in that country something had gone wrong with the appetite for food?

And would not anyone who had grown up in a different world think there was something equally queer about the state of the sex instinct among us?

C.S. Lewis, Mere Christianity

two. knowing.

The movie *500 Days of Summer,* is about a guy named Tom who falls in love with a girl named Summer. In the middle of the movie, Tom tells Summer:

> I need to know you're not going to wake up in the morning and feel differently about me.

I don't know your definition of beautiful, delightful, joyful, precious and good but I would say that Tom wanted something beautiful.

The name of the episode was "Boys will be Boys.[1] The description of the show was "Three guys have agreed to break a historic code of silence and help us unravel the mysteries of the male mind."

Amberlee was the girl's name and Justin was her former boyfriend. Since the show was revealing the mysteries of the male mind, Amberlee had an important question she wanted an answer for. When she had first started dating Justin, she had told him he had to stop going to strip clubs. She moved in with him, found a receipt for a strip club a little while later and then broke up with him.

Her question was "If I'm going to do it for free and there are no rules, why does he need to go somewhere else?"

I don't know your definition of beautiful, delightful, joyful, precious and good but I would say that Amberlee was asking a question that had something to do with delightful.

Marlow and Frances Cowan live in Iowa. They went to the Mayo Clinic in 2009 for a checkup and ended up performing a piano duet in the lobby of the clinic together. The video of that performance has been viewed over 2 million times. Marlow and Frances have been married 62 years.[2]

I don't know your definition of beautiful, delightful, joyful, precious and good but I would say that Marlow and Frances, in that video, show us something precious and good and beautiful.

There was a television show on Spring Breaks around the world. There were video clips of college students pouring beer on their bodies and girls in wet t-shirts. There were also clips of couples having sex on beaches, in hotel rooms, on boats, in clubs, on lawns, and a lot of other places that I don't remember. It seemed like everyone was having sex with anyone they could find and they were screaming things like "get naked" and "oox" and "have fun" into the camera while they lifted their shirts, stuck out their tongues, and drank beer, tequila, or whatever else, while their friends yelled and hollered and cheered.

One guy said, "I'm tri-sexual; I'll try anything sexual."

As I was sitting there watching, I started to have a small pity party for myself. Everyone on the television seemed like they were having a really good time – maybe even the time of their life. I started to ask myself questions.

> Why didn't I ever go to Cancun?
>
> Why didn't I get drunk and have sex with drunk girls on beaches and in boats and in clubs?
>
> Why didn't I come home with the satisfaction of having great sex with a bunch of women and knowing I'd never have to see them again?

Then I started to ask myself other questions.

> Is that beautiful, delightful, joyful, precious and good?
>
> Is that what you really want?
>
> Really?

MTV and the Associated Press carried out a fairly large survey. They asked teenagers what makes them happy. They replied that more than any other thing, family relationships make them happy.

Family relationships? What about Cancun?

knowing

In that same survey, 13 to 17-year-olds said that sex makes them *less* happy.

In the same survey, 18 to 24-year-olds said sex makes them happy for a moment but in the long term it makes them less happy.[3]

So ... a majority of teenagers said that eventually sex make them less happy.

Less happy? Less happy is not beautiful, delightful, joyful, precious or good. Even in Cancun.

mediocre
Seth Godin is a very smart man and one of my favorite thinkers and authors. He says this:

> Mediocre is merely a failed attempt to be really good.[4]

Remember Tom's beautiful question. Will you feel the same in the morning?

Summer replies:

> I can't give you that, no one can.

She can't?

Remember Amberlee's question? Why do you need to see someone else naked?

I picked up some books at the library. One of them was called *What Men Want*. I was pretty sure I already knew what men wanted, but I gave it a read anyway because I thought they might answer Amberlee's question. They did.

> Men also need variety in their lives. As we've said, if his woman is tall and blond, he will stare at that pretty petite brunette as if he'd just gotten out of prison. Looking at different women satisfies his visual imagination ... Understanding a man's desire to go to a strip bar will improve your relationship with your boyfriend. First

THE NAKED FRUIT

> of all, professional men think it is "cool" when their girlfriends do not have a problem with their going.[5]

Remember Marlow and Frances? Do they need variety? Sixty-two years together is a long time.

There are a lot of people who look like they are having fun in Cancun only to come home and admit they really aren't that happy.

It seems like beautiful, delightful, joyful, precious and good are right there.

Right there and we just ... can't ... seem ... to ... grab ... them.

> Mediocre is merely a failed attempt to be really good.

Neuroscientists say we have a flaw in our brain: a flaw, I would say, even showed up with Eve in that story.

> This failing is rooted in our emotions, which tend to overvalue immediate gains at the cost of future expenses. Our feelings are thrilled by the prospect of an immediate reward, but they can't really grapple with the long-term fiscal consequences of that decision.[6]

Eve thought the fruit looked good and so she took a bite. She probably thought she had made a good choice, at first. I'm sure it must have tasted good, just like she had imagined. She had time to recommend it to Adam and convince him it was worth the bite.

After she put on clothes, and saw weeds, and had strange desires she had never had before, she probably would have agreed with all those MTV teenagers: happy in the short term but less happy in the long term.

Is that it? We're mediocre because we have a flaw in our brain?

donuts

Three other men and I meet every other week at a place called *The Donut Parade*. *The Donut Parade* has been around a long time. Its walls have heard plenty of conversations about sports, politics, sex knowing

and everything else, I'm sure. The formica below the bar stools is worn. The ceiling tiles are stained with donut grease and whatever else finds its way to ceiling tiles to stain them. About half of the fluorescent bulbs work which means it's almost dark at our table, especially in the winter.

But, *The Donut Parade* is cheap. Three dollars for our handmade maple bars (still steaming when we get them) and five refills of watered down coffee that somehow tastes good – and that includes a dollar tip. It's a perfect spot to hang out with three guys and talk about ourselves, our lives, and what makes us tick.

We talk about a lot of things, including Cancun. We talk about MTV polls. We talk about short term versus the long term. We talk about Adolf Hitler.

Adolf Hitler once said:

> Make the lie big, make it simple, keep saying it, and eventually they will believe it.

We think there are a lot of lies out there. We often feel like we're fighting the lies or in some kind of war and every time we do the things that the lies say we should do, we, like the teenagers in that poll, aren't very happy. We think we get glimpses of beautiful, delightful, joyful, precious and good and when we do, we want more.

We think there might a failing in our brain but we also think someone is lying to us and convincing us of the short-term and sometimes we believe them.

We're trying to figure out ourselves and our desires. We're trying to figure out what is true and what isn't. We're trying to understand how that nasty-smelling smoke has sunk into our clothes, just like donut grease does.

We're trying to figure out if we believe things because they are repeated and simple or because they are true.

daughters
Daughters are an interesting thing. Three of us donut boys have

THE NAKED FRUIT

daughters; I have two. Daughters make you think about a lot of things, including the future. Daughters make you think about individual futures and the future of societies.

I once watched a video shot in the red-light district of Amsterdam.[7] Amsterdam has legal prostitution and they rent out tiny one-bedroom apartments to prostitutes who stand in the windows inviting visitors to come inside, pay a few bucks, and have their way with their STD-free (they are checked regularly) bodies.

The men in the video I watched were pretty excited about being in such a lovely garden of fresh fruits and, really, who can blame them? The fault in their brain was running wild and immediate thrills of all sizes and shapes and nationalities surrounded them. However, when the interviewer in the video asked them if they would want their daughter in those windows, everything changed. The fruit changed and the long-term consequences started to come into view. The smiles shifted to frowns and the rush of passion was suddenly not so raging. One man answered, with the windows and silhouettes behind him:

> I think you should always think, what if it's your daughter up there? That's something people should consider.

Right, what if that was my daughter up there? What if it was my daughter dancing around the pole? What if it was my daughter on the boat in Cancun? What if Amberlee was my daughter?

When you ask most guys what they would do if their daughter's boyfriend did to their daughter what they did to girls they dated, they will answer with words like "shotgun," "bastard," and "kill." Country singers love to sing about carrying shotguns around when their daughters start dating. I heard a story of an ex-Marine who said that any boy that wants to date his daughter has to first take him on a date. There's a reason most dads are scared to death of their daughter's dating – they know what they were like when they dated.

For some reason when a daughter is in the picture the smoke of the lies starts to clear. Maybe the innocence, purity, and beauty of a woman suddenly slaps us in the face like it never has before. Maybe the potential for harm is suddenly so clear. Maybe we start to see true value instead of sexual value. Maybe we see how perfect they are, and

knowing

yet we know what lies ahead. Maybe we see, in the face of a 10 year old girl, beauty, joy, delight, precious, and good.

Maybe daughters indicate that it's possible for us to overcome that failing in our brain and think long term.

Maybe we see a little bit of Eve in our daughters and we realize that the same story is about to be played out again, with a fresh start and we have a moment to hope that the ending changes.

If there are fresh starts, that means there are still places with beauty, joy, delight, precious and good things.

enemies
There is a Chinese proverb which says:

> So it is said that if you know your enemies and know yourself, you can win a thousand battles without a single loss. If you only know yourself, but not your opponent, you may win or may lose. If you know neither yourself nor your enemy, you will always endanger yourself.

Is there an enemy? Do we know who this enemy is? Do we know ourselves? Do we know how this enemy has affected us?

It seems as though we need to know. If we don't, we're going to continue to fail at this thing and we're all going to see less good and more screwed up.

It seems like we already are.

Maybe if we look at some of the messed up, we'll start to get a better grasp on our enemy. Maybe if we get a better grasp on our enemy, we'll start to know our enemy and ourselves and then, just maybe, we can win a thousand battles without a single loss.

That sounds good to me.

Maybe the words aren't that important. It's like, I know he really cares about me, you know, even if he can't say if he does. And yeah, he always talks about sex, but that's ok 'cause he's a guy, right?

Vicki, American Pie

three. skin with a twist.

According to reports:

Seventy percent of men think about sex at least once a day.[1]

Fifty-four percent of pastors have viewed porn in the last year.[2]

Strip clubs generate $5 billion of revenue every year in the U.S.[3]

Porn revenue is greater than all combined revenues of all professional football, baseball and basketball franchises.[4]

Domestic revenues for pornography are larger than the revenues of Microsoft, Google, Amazon, eBay, Yahoo!, Apple, Netflix and Earthlink combined.[5]

I don't think we need statistics to prove that there is a strong correlation between sex and men. According to some psychologists, sex is the number one "need" of a man.[6]

That word, need.

If sex is the number one need of a man, than my question is why do men do so many things that aren't sex? If you look at the statistics again, you start to notice that none of them actually deal with men participating in sex.

There is *thinking* about sex. There is *looking* at sex, or at least some form of it, on a computer, in a magazine or on a movie. There is *watching* a woman dancing sexually, taking off her clothes and maybe sitting on a lap but still ...

Do thinking, looking, and watching ever satisfy anything? Really?

Don't get me wrong. I realize there are plenty of statistics that indicate our participation in sex, but with so much watching and simulating and looking and imagining, you have to wonder what the affects are.

THE NAKED FRUIT

What kind of an affect does all this thinking, looking, simulating and watching have on us in terms of our expectations of sex and in terms of how we treat sex when we finally get around to actually having sex?

I sometimes wonder what Adam would think of all our thinking, looking, watching and imagining if he were to show up today. "You're still listening to that snake?"

Snakes
They are an interesting animal.

There are some who say that we, as humans, tend to not like snakes precisely because of the story of Adam and Eve. The story has been drilled into us so many times that we subsequently view snakes as evil and something to stay away from.

I don't know why I don't like snakes and don't really spend that much time figuring out why. I just know I don't.

History tells me I'm not alone. Humans have always had an issue with snakes. Rarely are snakes the good guy. In fact, they are usually the bad guy. No matter the culture, all those stories, myths, legends, fables and drawings about dragons, leviathans and other lizard-snake things that live in oceans and caves, and will eat you when you go near them, are often very similar. It's not a coincidence.

Many cultures view snakes as demons. Many as devils. Many just plain evil.

> Sociologists sometimes say that groups can exist without a god, but no group can exist without a devil.[7]

Snakes are often the visual representation of evil.

Maybe that's all the snake in the story ever was.

If I step back and take a look at everything going on around me, it's not a stretch to think that there is something evil messing with our heads today. I can't help but wonder if we really are carrying around a bit of that evil in our mind, our imagination, and our soul. When evil enters, it permeates, and when it permeates it sticks around from generation to generation, and when it sticks around from generation to generation, it has more of an influence even as it becomes less obvious.

I find that very scary. As it gains influence, its influence becomes less obvious.

mediocre
What if evil has embodied mediocrity?

What if mediocrity is our devil?

What if mediocrity is becoming more and more influential even while we accept mediocrity as more and more normal?

Wouldn't that be scary?

Mediocrity, as Seth Godin said, is a failed attempt to be really good. A mediocre athlete wanted to be really good but ended up, instead ...

>just like everyone else.

Evil loves mediocrity. Evil hates really good. Mediocrity is a great substitute for really good because it's just enough good that it fools us all enough so we stop trying for really good.

We become satisfied with mediocrity.

Taking the best and giving us a cheap imitation. That is what drives mediocrity. Seeing us accept anything but the finest, makes mediocrity smile every time. Mediocrity is smart, he is cunning, and he is powerful.

Mediocrity is our enemy.

Maybe that's why we are settling for all this fake stuff. Maybe every time we settle for the fake stuff, we end up making the real thing a little more mediocre and we don't even realize it.

naked
From the time I can remember I was taken to church every Sunday.

THE NAKED FRUIT

That means from the time I was little I was told about something called morality. A lot of people don't have time for morality because morality says that there are wrong things and right things. Most of us, me included, don't like being told that we can't decide what's wrong and right for ourselves, especially if the things we are told are wrong provide some thrills.

Regardless, one of the things that I was taught was wrong was looking at naked women on paper, on screens, and in real life, if they weren't my wife. I don't remember if I was given a lot of reasons why it was wrong, but I was told that I shouldn't do it.

I have quite a few friends who grew up in the church too. I could count off a long list of them if you wanted me to. Many of them were taught to believe the same as I do on this topic.

So here's the weird thing. Just about every single one of us *has* looked at naked women on paper, on screens, and in real life, who weren't our wives. We were all raised with the impression it was wrong and harmful and yet we have done it, or do it now, regardless of what we were raised to believe.

I often ask myself why.

> Maybe we don't believe it's wrong anymore?
>
> Maybe it doesn't matter whether we think it's wrong or not, we just can't resist?
>
> Maybe we don't know why?

Why is naked skin so damn powerful?

I think it's very hard for women to understand how much men desire to see them naked. Men like naked women so much that, as the statistics show, they look at pictures of naked women and get turned on.

Think about that for a second.

We look at pictures of women we have never met, will never meet, will never have a relationship with, will never touch, will never kiss, will

skin with a twist

never have sex with – and get turned on.

That's amazing if you think about it.

Men get such a thrill from a nudity that they will pay more money than just about any other industry for the thrill. Hugh Hefner knows this very well.[8] Men will pay money, and lots of it, to see any form of nudity on screen, on paper, or in real life at a strip club. Men hoot and holler not because they are going to have sex with the woman but because they are going to see her naked or watch her have sex with another man.

Really?

Men, you could say, *crave* naked women.

When I was in sixth grade I came across my first naked woman. In fact it was multiple naked women in the form of a big stack of Playboy magazines that a friend had. It was Christmas in July. In fact, the top magazine had a lady dressed up as Santa Claus. She was a lot thinner and had bigger boobs than the Santa I had known up to that point, but she was wearing the red coat and red hat – at least partially.

Something drew me to those magazines. Something tingled when I looked at them. It was as though I couldn't resist their magnetic pull. I can still see that Santa. What's crazy to me, looking back, is that I was in sixth grade. I have a kid who is in eighth grade right now. I was staring at some woman in a magazine that I would never know nor see in real life and even if I did I would have no idea what to do with her. She could have been old enough to be my mom, and she didn't have any reindeer with her. I stared and stared and felt giddy and happy and turned the pages.

You can't help but ask why, why, why.

chemicals
The experts say that hormones start flowing around fourth or fifth grade and they keep going and going and going, for men and for women. I'm not sure when they officially stop, but they do slow down a little ... eventually.

At least, I think.

THE NAKED FRUIT

Until the early twenties, these hormones are coming so strong that, in my opinion, a boy has to consciously remember to use his mind. Up to that point, hormones are running the remote controls on the drones.

Some people say boys don't have brains. Turns out those "some people" are scientists who study the brain. More accurately, they say young boys, amped up on hormones, don't have some parts of their brains:

> Brain areas that are relatively recent biological inventions — such as the frontal lobes — don't finish growing until the teenage years are over ... Teens make bad decisions because they are literally less rational.[9]

We've established that we already have a fault in our brain that prevents us from seeing the long term. Now we're saying that young men, running on hormones, have an amplified fault: they can hardly make rational decisions.

That seems like it could be a problem.

Parents, of course, are often aware of this problem and create leashes and saddles to rein in the hormones and limit the exposure to forbidden fruits. These are most often known as rules. Of course the problem with rules is the same problem we have with morality: We don't like to be told what is wrong or right or what we can or cannot do, especially when our brains can barely understand reason, let alone the reasons for the rules.

Some parents respond with things like "it's more important for hormones to be restrained than esteems to be boosted."[10]

Some kids respond to those parents with things like "you suck".

Regardless, think about these creatures we call boys/men for a moment. Maybe you are one. Maybe you were one. Maybe you know one. Maybe you are dating one.

They are run by hormones that feed them emotional thrills upon seeing nudity. They lack the ability to understand any long-term consequences that could come from these thrills. They are told over and over by

skin with a twist

everyone that these thrills are good and should be pursued so what little reasoning ability they do have is being twisted the wrong direction.

If anyone is telling them they shouldn't pursue these thrills with all of their being, it is their parents, who are setting up rules which no one likes, and that makes them want to disobey all the more. This is all happening from roughly the early teens to the early twenties – the prime dating years.

In other words, these are the kinds of people girls most often date.

1 in 5 of them is sending or receiving nude or semi-nude pictures on their cell phone.[11] These creatures spend an average of 87 hours a year looking at naked women online.[12]

I suppose it makes perfect sense that they grow up to spend all that money and spend all that time focused on ways to see more naked women …

Dr. Sari Locker, a sex educator and professor of adolescent psychology at Columbia University, says this:

> When boys receive a nude picture of a girl, they think the next time they see her they can go further with her in a sexual way than before. It becomes an invitation to advance a sexual relationship.[13]

Nudity is an invitation. That starts to make sense why we're so enthralled with it.

I would like to ask Dr. Sari Locker if the invitation only applies to the naked woman that we are looking at or simply the next woman we happen to hang out with.

I bet mediocrity knows.

faux
While I was in college one of my friends and I went to visit some other friends at a smaller school. While we there, for some reason, someone started bragging about masturbation. I don't have a problem bragging about some things, but masturbating is not one of them. It's not as

though any guy in the world can't do what you are bragging about – which really means you can't act like you are cooler than everyone else, and thus I don't get the bragging.

Regardless, those guys started talking about masturbating on a tractor while plowing the fields, masturbating while driving, while flying, while doing homework, watching television, movies, reading – if you can think of it, chances are, they said it. One guy I know was proud of the fact that he had masturbated in every building on our college campus. (I went to a big school.)

Why do guys brag about masturbating?

95 percent of guys have masturbated at some point in their life. If you tried to think of other things that 95 percent of men have done, I'm not sure you can find many. I've personally never met a guy who has never masturbated.

Now some of this is common and natural. You're thirteen, you start discovering new things about your body, and yeah, we all get it.

I get that.

My concern is that we are starting to blend the line between masturbating and sex. I thought we all knew that while it might be closer to sex than looking at some pictures, we still knew it wasn't sex.

But given all the bragging, I start to wonder.

I don't know if it's wrong or right in terms of morality, but I do know that pulling down your pants and having some alone time with yourself is not equal with having sex.

But it seems as though not everyone agrees with me: people like John Mayer.[14]

> Playboy: Masturbation for you is as good as sex?
>
> Mayer: Absolutely, because during sex, I'm just going to run a filmstrip. I'm still masturbating. That's what you do when you're 30, 31, 32. This is my problem now:

> Rather than meet somebody new, I would rather go home and replay the amazing experiences I've already had.
>
> Playboy: You'd rather jerk off to an ex-girlfriend than meet someone new?
>
> Mayer: Yeah. What that explains is that I'm more comfortable in my imagination than I am in actual human discovery. The best days of my life are when I've dreamed about a sexual encounter with someone I've already been with. When that happens, I cannot lay off myself.

I've heard a radio host say that men view urinals as a depository for urine and women as a depositary for semen.[15] I've read a book in which the author called sorority girls "a convenient receptacle for my ejaculate".[16]

Apparently, it's a fine line between masturbating with yourself and masturbating in a girl.

Or, not so fine.

You hear those kinds of things and wonder how many men would agree with the statements and what statements like those mean to our view of sex and our view of women and our movement away from beautiful, joyful, delightful, precious and good.

If the result of spending a day walking through a park hand in hand, going out to dinner, seeing a movie, returning home and slowly undressing one another and kissing, fondling, unzipping, whatever else, and eventually having sex is the same as a guy and his hand for 60 seconds …

> What does that mean for all of us?

According to C.S. Lewis:

> … [W]e say, of a lustful man prowling the streets that he "wants a woman." Strictly speaking, a woman is

> just what he does not want. He wants a pleasure for which a woman happens to be the necessary piece of apparatus. How much he cares about the woman as such may be gauged by his attitude to her five minutes after fruition (one does not keep the carton after one has smoked the cigarettes).[17]

I love so many parts of that quote.

A lustful man doesn't want a woman, he wants an apparatus to help him ejaculate. He wants a fancy hand. If a woman is simply a fancy hand then, Lewis goes on, a man will treat her like a carton of cigarettes after the hand has done what it needed to do.

I'm not sure where you stand on morals and rules but, if you are a woman, or you care about any woman on planet earth, that should not seem like a good result to you.

C.S. Lewis again.

> You must not suppose that this was romantic passion. The passion of my life … belonged to a wholly different region. What I felt for the dancing mistress was sheer appetite; the prose and not the poetry of the Flesh.[18]

If all this thinking, looking, watching, and simulating leads to more sheer appetites and treating women like cartons of cigarettes, why are we spending so much money to do it?

Maybe mediocrity knows.

driving
Lots of statistics. Hormones. Cartons of cigarettes.

What does it all mean?

Where are we going?

What road are we traveling down?

Mediocrity is everywhere. The lies are simple, loud, and everywhere.

skin with a twist

The lies are also appealing. They have to be.
Enemies are never as stupid as we want them to be.

If the fruit looked rotten from the beginning, no one would ever eat it. The lies have to look good. The lies have to offer us some short term thrills in order to hide the long term consequences.

It's a system. It's a road we're all traveling down, contributing to, gaining speed. We're all participating in the system, at some level or another.

We're all pressing the accelerator or the brake.

Men *need* to go to strip clubs.

Men *need* to satisfy their visual imagination.

They sound so innocent and fine. Even good. In fact, there are doctors, psychologists, sex therapists and every other kind of expert who will confirm that the statements are true and noble and beneficial.

Of course, they will. There are billions of dollars at play. There are always experts who will gladly fight for mediocrity.

And all the while we're blazing down the road as the hormones, the brain faults, the desires, the watching, the thinking, and the simulating add up, one little choice on another, gaining speed all the way to ...

Where?

Have you heard about the growing prostitution trade in Iraq? Amidst the war zone, there are many Iraqi widows who are selling their bodies for as little as $20 a night for sex with those who will pay. In one story, one of these women was having sex while three of her children were standing in the room, staring into the corners, while their mom tried to earn a living.[19]

Make the lie big, make it simple, keep saying it, and eventually they will believe it.

What are we believing?

THE NAKED FRUIT

> Outside the IZ you can get a girl for the evening for $25 ... Many Iraqi women are gorgeous, and, since there is nothing that really resembles a functional economy, some of them are up for screwing to support themselves and their five kids. I ended up getting some girls from an Iraqi security contractor ... I was EXTREMELY stupid, LUCKY, and DRUNK one nite when I took a taxi around downtown Baghdad looking for women. I met a pimp and he took me to a house where I banged 3 girls for 60 bucks until I heard morning prayers.
>
> She wasn't hot, but NO man is turning down p---- in Iraq. I took her back to my trailer, gave her some whiskey (her first alcohol ever), and we had a wild few hours. Arab women – at least this one was – are very submissive in bed and you can really have your way with them.
>
> Damn the IED's, anal sex with Persian girls makes it worth it.[20]

Lots of invitations.

Eventually, the needs, the desires, the variety, the thinking, the watching, the simulating leads to a sheer appetite, regardless of whether her kids are there or not.

Eventually, she's a cartons of cigarettes and better if she is a submissive carton.

Mediocrity knows this.

I'm not hooking up with prostitutes, you argue. Seeing a girl in a strip club is hardly the same.

You're in the system.

We all are. Which direction are you driving us?

Are you moving us toward beautiful, delightful, precious, joyful and good ... or away from it?

skin with a twist

These are the extremes, you respond. These are the worst of the worst.

Maybe.

Or maybe, as Peter Rollins said:

> Most often the major temptation we face is not connected with some extreme act, but the temptation to give in to mediocrity.[21]

Being a woman is a terribly difficult task, since it consists principally in dealing with men.

Joseph Conrad

four. women.

Beautiful.
Delightful.
Joyful.
Precious.
Good.

One thing in the story, actually, was not good. There was a problem.

Before Eve came along the man was alone. Adam was lonely. He had lots of friends but none of them made everything beautiful, delightful, joyful, precious, and good.

But then she showed up and his whole world changed.

I'd love to know what he did the first time he saw her. The look of awe. The dropped jaw. The wide eyes. The smile. But, he didn't write any songs or poems or speeches.

In fact, the story goes, he said this:

> This is now bone of my bones and flesh of my flesh.[1]

Bone of my bones and flesh of my flesh.

If I was going to make sure that history knew one thing I thought of my wife, I'm not sure that would be it.

Bone of my bones and flesh of my flesh?

But, the more you look at it, the more you read it, the more you think about it ...

> the more incredible it becomes.

Why?
> He realized she was a part of him.

THE NAKED FRUIT

>He realized that when she was hurt, he was hurt.
>
>When she was happy, he was happy.
>
>When she was satisfied, he was satisfied.
>
>When she was upset, he was upset.
>
>When she ... he .

She was him: His bones and his flesh. His substance. His nakedness.

Him.

He realized there was a connection between the two of them. He realized that there was something deeper and meaningful and beautiful that bound them together. Adam realized that she was a part of him and he was a part of her.

The more I think about it, the more beautiful, delightful, joyful, precious, and good those lines are.

You are me. I am you.

Men have written all kinds of things about women ever since the story of Adam and Eve. Some of them are really nice of some of them are not:

>I have found it impossible to carry the heavy burden of responsibility and to discharge my duties as king as I would wish to do without the help of the woman I love.
>-Edward VIII
>
>The most precious possession that ever comes to a man in this world is a woman's heart.
>-Timothy Titcomb
>
>No coffee dates, no lunch dates. These are non-humping dates. You want their inhibitions a little lower. You want them to feel like something is expected of them. Your chances for getting laid increase dramatically. Nobody

> ever got laid after a coffee-shop date. There's no point in going.
>
> You want to minimize the distance from drinking to sex. If she asks you to stop at a fast-food restaurant, or diner, she's stalling (filibustering). She knows she's a little buzzed and is trying to buy some time to sober up. Sober up so she won't be as horny and try to avoid sleeping with you.
>
> Never compliment a woman. It raises her self-esteem and will probably lessen your chance of getting laid.
> -Tom Leykis[2]

Bone of my bones *to*
                    never compliment a woman.

The most precious possession in the world *to*
                    a means to an end.

A Canadian study on date rape indicated that 60% of Canadian men would commit sexual assault if they were sure they wouldn't get caught.[3]

How do we move from a precious treasure to something we would rape if we wouldn't get caught? Or, judging from the statistics that say 20 to 25% of college women are raped during their college career,[4] maybe we rape them whether we'll get caught or not.

How did we get there?

What leads a radio host to say men should never compliment a woman because that raises her self-esteem and if you have a woman with a high self-esteem you probably won't get laid?

Maybe these are the extremes? If so, what are the averages?

Maybe there are a few consistent things with men and the way they look at women. Maybe it's in the few consistent things where we find how the lies have affected us, where we find how far we've come from him and her …

and beautiful, delightful, precious, joyful, and good ...to something else.

pennies

It was a bacholor party. We were all having dinner when the father-in-law-to-be began to talk about "titties". I don't remember all the details but I do remember this older married man talking a lot about strip clubs and a lot about "titties" while his 13-year-old son, and son-in-law sat at the table with him.

I don't care if you think strip clubs are cool. It's not cool to hear about them from a guy in his fifties who can't stop mentioning the word "titties". The word is weird enough already.

From there it moved to some advice to the 13-year-old to start "getting it" and to make sure to use a "jim-hat" and then some more compliments on the nice "titties" he remembered seeing.

Finally, we got to the "advice for the bachelor" stage of the evening: the sage words that all the drunk friends give to the guy about to get married. There were some nuggets and as wise as it all was, it generally came down to this: "Get it while you can."

On a vacation I met a man who was going to get married the next day. We were hanging out with our spouses (his spouse to-be) in a hot tub with a bottle of wine and a beautiful view. After talking about the celebration that was about to happen, he said, "Yeah, tomorrow, I get castrated."

I laughed but I'm not sure why. It's one of those jokes that is always said, isn't that funny, and yet everyone laughs.

There is an illustration that says if you put a penny into a jar for every time you have sex in your first year of marriage and then pull a penny out of the jar for every time you have sex after your first year of marriage, you'll never pull all of the pennies out of the jar.

I could go on but I think we get. This idea that a woman changes after you get married is everywhere, in some form or another. The hot and heavy dating days lead the way to the boring, cold, stale, sleep in separate bed days.

women

What the hell?

Who started this ridiculous idea and why do we keep repeating it at bachelor parties and laughing at jokes that bring it up?

prophets

Self-fulfilling prophecies are one of those weird and amazing phenomenon. They are all over classic literature, from Greek to Roman, to Macbeth by Shakespeare. The idea is that you know something is going to happen, you try to prevent it from happening and thus, it happens because you try to prevent it.

I wonder if we don't do the same thing in marriage. We believe we're not going to get it after we marry so we try as hard as we can and do whatever it takes to get it before we're married, never stopping to ask how much of that doing-whatever-it-takes-before-we-get-married comes back to affect our marriage and the sexual dynamics within it.

Apparently, there is a sex crisis in America.

The number of times Americans have sex is going down and psychologists estimate 1 in 5 marriages are sexless (sex less than 10 times a year).[5] While the report goes on to blame the problem on a bad diet, it doesn't make any mention of self-fulfilling prophecies.

Remember that teenagers said being sexually active made them less happy.[6] If you grow up equating sex with being less happy, then why would you want to have a lot of sex when you are married?

I mentioned the book What Men Want earlier. One of its "truths" about men was:

> If men didn't have to marry, we wouldn't …
>
> When a man considers marriage, the first thing he thinks about is not being able to have sex with other women … His whole body, his whole mind, his whole self recoils from this idea.

I wonder why men marry at all.

THE NAKED FRUIT

I wonder how much a woman wants to have sex with a man she is married to whom she knows just wants to have sex with other women.

I just heard a radio host talking about wives who let their husbands have sex with other women, as long as they don't find out about it. It's great for their marriage.

I wonder why a man would want to have sex with other women if he knew his wife would want to have sex with him.

I wonder if men thought they were going to get more sex *after* marriage than before it, if suddenly, that prophecy would start to be fulfilled too.

roses
There is now a whole style of story-telling that is known as "romantic comedy" or better, "chick flick". The story usually goes something like this:

> Boy meets girl.
>
> Something happens that might separate boy and girl.
>
> Boy and girl kiss in random scene.
>
> Boy and girl get mad at each other.
>
> Boy and girl come back together and kiss with sunset behind them.
>
> Romance and emotion are pouring out from the screen and everyone cries because they are sad and happy and love is everywhere.

There is another style of story-telling known as action flicks and they usually go something like this:

> Guy with major muscles. Worked out for six months to get the role.
>
> Bad dialogue.

women

> Muscle guy has to save world.
>
> First he meets sexy actress in a tight shirt.
>
> Explosions.
>
> Fighting.
>
> Sex in a shower or the rain.
>
> More battles.
>
> Wicked triumphant end scene where muscle man has sex with sexy actress while the evil guy's car/army/headquarters blows up in the background.

It's been said many times that women tend to be more "feeling" and men tend to be more "logical." Women "reflect" and men "act."

I don't know if a man was the one who created the generalizations, but I'm pretty sure that most men would agree with them at some level or another, even though, scientifically, both genders do a lot of both.

If men think these things about women, they most definitely bring these thoughts into the world of sex. We bring most of our thoughts there and when we bring this feeling-versus-thinking thought it goes something like this:

> Women are feeling.
>
> Flowers make women feel good inside.
>
> When women feel good inside it affects their emotions and makes them happy.
>
> When women are made happy, they are also happy toward the person that made them happy.
>
> When women are happy toward you they will have sex with you much easier.

THE NAKED FRUIT

> Therefore, buy women flowers in order to have sex with them.

Romance is a funny thing. Webster's say it is "inclined toward or suggestive of the feeling of the excitement and mystery associated with love."

Men tend to focus on what those feelings – that excitement and mystery – will mean for them. Men tend to think that if a woman has the feeling of love, that feeling will pay dividends for him.

Men spend a good bit of time deducing new ways to trigger feelings of excitement of love, and romance so that it's harder to resist – jewelry, flowers, dinners, scenic views, picnics and sometimes engagement rings.

Mediocrity, of course, knows this.

> He spent a lot of money on that jewelry. Are you really going to tell him to get his hands off you?
>
> Are you really going to let her tell you to get your hands off her?

Robert Cialdini is a social psychologist who wrote in one of his books about the rule of reciprocation. It is a psychological tendency of all humans to give back.

> The rule says that we should try to repay, in kind, what another person has provided us. If a woman does us a favor, we should do her one in return ... the rule possesses awesome strength, often producing a "yes" response to a request that, except for an existing feeling of indebtedness, would surely have been refused.[7]

In the same way a salesperson will give a potential client a free sample to make them feel indebted to buy something, a man will give an object to make a woman feel indebted to give something in return even if, under normal circumstances, she would have said no.

Cialdini says that she is more likely to be committed to that choice and give in again, because of another rule of human behavior.[8] In other words, the gift doesn't need to be as big the next time, because we have committed to a sense of indebtedness to the sales person or boyfriend.

If you have ever seen a person stuck in a bad relationship, you might understand a little more of why now.

Another "rule" of human behavior is the rule of commitment and consistency.

Cialdini again:

> Once we have made a choice or taken a stand, we will encounter personal and interpersonal pressures to behave consistently with that commitment.[9]

So all of this comes back to a common thing we see in men. They think they are not going to get sex after marriage so they need to get all they can before marriage. Men believe that because women are more affected by emotion, they will use emotion to their own advantage before marriage. They will be romantic, they will create situations that are harder for a woman to resist, they will think of ways to make her feel as though she must reciprocate knowing that once she has reciprocated once or twice, it will take less and less to cause her to do it again and again.

In short, some men use women.

Men may have never heard of Robert Cialdini but trust me, they know the rules.

Then men get married and suddenly lose what romantic ability they had because the prophecy says they are not going to have sex anymore and because the lies tell them they need variety.

Women who marry these men participate in a huge emotional, romantic event that provides much of the emotional feedback the woman was seeking all along. If she was only having sex to receive that, well, she suddenly has lost one of her main motivations to have sex.

So, she is less likely to respond to a guy who is less likely to give and ... even more of a self-fulfilling prophecy because the whole relationship, up to that point, has been built on lies, deception and mediocrity.

Have you ever seen that story?

On a lesser, more common, scale, men start to be less romantic because half of the reason they were romantic was to have as much sex before marriage as possible because it won't happen after marriage. And why be romantic after marriage since there isn't going to be much sex anyway and that was the main motivator?

Have you ever seen that story?

orphans
It was made for disaster. A nation with strict abortion and birth control laws, incentives for having children, and extreme economic depression and poverty. The result was thousands of orphans, many of them in atrocious settings.

Babies were placed in cribs and never touched, or rarely touched, for the first years of life. Children in many of these orphanages were only given five to six minutes of attention a day. As a result, reports say that 1 out of every 10 will end up in psychiatric institutions and all of them will suffer severe trauma.[10]

It's a tragic story but illustrates well the fact that we all need love and things go wrong when we don't get it.

For some reason, men often think women need love more and so we have created a popular saying that goes something like this:

> Men will give love to get sex and women will give sex to get love.

The statement implies two different desires for the two different genders: sex for men and love for women. It also implies that each of us will give something to the opposite gender in order to get what we want. It doesn't necessarily imply that sex is not important to her and love not important to him, but it does give some indication of priority, or at least of the end goal.

Statistics agree to some degree ... that she needs love, often of a male figure, more specifically a father. She will be affected by how much love she receives by a male figure, in the same way orphans are affected by how much attention they receive. Some research says that a woman who grows up in a single-mother home is five times more likely to become a teen mom than a girl growing up in a home with both parents.[11]

We already know men want sex.

Either way, there are a wide variety of men and women who participate in this give and take of sex and love:

Some women make sure they are getting love before they give sex.

Some women are so desperate for love they will give sex for any hint of love.

Some men will truly give love and sex is a nice benefit.

Some men will only give love to get sex and some will only give the smallest amounts of love needed in order to get the most sex needed.

Wherever we are on the scale it seems that love, sex, and deal should never be in the same sentence.

When two people are giving something in order to get something are either of them really giving the best of anything?

> The best way to get approval is not to need it.[12]

I like that. The best way to get some things is not to be desperate for them.

What are porn stars desperate for? Strippers? Drunk girls in Cancun?

Are they getting it?

Are men pretending to give it in order to get something else?

THE NAKED FRUIT

Is anyone winning with any of these games?

Mediocrity knows.

worlds
There is this scene in the amazing television series *Planet Earth* that documents the mating ritual of the rare Bird of Paradise. The cameraman crouched behind a tree for days at a time, waiting for this little bird to do his thing. When the little guy finally did, it was stunning.

A blue-feathered creature popped out of the jungle and onto a tree trunk. An enormous fan opened around its head and he began hopping up and down trying to prove to the female that he was what she needed to go home with. He was literally dancing, showing his best moves and dressed in his best clothes.

Sometimes we talk about how we should be more like animals. Sometimes we talk about how further evolved we are.

I'm not sure we are actually that different.

My wife and I were on a trip to New York City. We were at a little restaurant that you can only find in New York, with that energy that only New York seems to have. We ate dinner with some friends and as the dinner was winding down the restaurant began to wind up. We didn't realize that at ten the hip restaurant turned into a hip club. The music started pumping, the singles started arriving, and we were in a prime little happening spot in the city on a Friday night.

We were like that cameraman. Instead of hiding for days, we just had to eat a good dinner.

But we both witnessed a mating ritual.

The first few brave souls hit the dance floor and began to break it down. There was a cute girl and her friend. Her friend was also cute but not nearly as "unrestrained." You know the one. She was grinding on some guy within minutes.

Another guy and girl were doing the cool, "Walk and dance while holding a drink" moves, pretending to be too cool to really let it all out.

As we watched, we hypothesized the relationships between the girls and guys, and the friends, and whether or not they would go home to one of those guys' apartment and have sex that night.

My wife eventually said this:

> "I really don't think girls realize what they are doing."
>
> "What do you mean?" I asked.
>
> "Well, I mean, that girl doesn't know what she's doing to him. She's having a good time and he's… well, he's thinking more than that. She's just here for fun and –"
>
> "No way," I interrupted. "Are you telling me she comes to the bar for a fun time and happens to end up in his apartment because she doesn't realize what she's doing to him?"
>
> "Well, no, I'm not saying that. I'm just saying she doesn't understand the consequences of her actions."
>
> "As in what way? She doesn't know she's turning him on?" I asked.
>
> "No, she doesn't. She doesn't know what he's thinking."
>
> "Babe, c'mon."
>
> My wife sighed and tried one more time to explain. "She's dancing, having fun. She's wearing some clothes that make her look hot for her friends. This guy is looking at the sexy clothes, thinking she is wearing them so that he can take them off, and the guy is looking at the sexy moves, thinking she is busting them out because she wants to go home with him. She doesn't get what she's doing to him. I didn't."

Two different worlds: one that guys live in and one that girls live in.

THE NAKED FRUIT

We talked on the plane ride home about whether or not either one of them was good, delightful, joyful, precious and beautiful.

My wife remembers being sixteen very well. She remembers the hilarious fights with her dad about the bikini. She remembers her dad saying, "I know how guys are" and "I know what guys are thinking".

She remembers thinking her dad had no idea what he was talking about. She couldn't comprehend what he was saying.

"I do now," she has said a few times.

One of my friends was telling me about the hot new receptionist that showed up at his office. She wore some sexy tight jeans to work one day, so the men came up with a plan. One guy would go up to the receptionist and ask her to get something out of one of the lower drawers while another guy would be perfectly positioned to see the booty as she bent over.

The boys played the game for a while, getting the best angle and view amidst the laughs and brow-raises.

On the surface, it's harmless. If you're the receptionist it's even flattering that the men think your butt is so fine that they want to look at it with their buddies over and over. That's her world.

The guys, after playing the game, said they were remembering her bending over for the "spank bank" later on.

That's his world.

Most guys are not especially eager to tell a woman what they think about as they simulate sex in their heads. Sometimes, like John Mayer, it's a past experience. Sometimes it's the girl on the beach, the girl in the grocery store, or the girl at the gym.

Sometimes it's just imagining taking those tight jeans off, lifting the sexy shirt over her head or untying the skim bikini that you saw earlier in the day while in the grocery store line, waiting to get a coffee or at the club.

women

I followed a link to the some Polaroid eyewear ads.[13] There are three of them, styled like a little comic strip.

The first shows a guy in the car with his girlfriend and in the back seat is a girl with a low-cut shirt. The guy checks out the girl's cleavage in his rearview mirror, his girlfriend sees him do it, and he gets slapped.

However, with the Polaroid sunglasses on (which it shows in the next frame) the guy can stare at the girl's cleavage and his girlfriend gives him a kiss at the end of the day (because she can't tell he's staring at the girl) with the words "Yeah Cool."

The other two follow similar lines: a guy checking out the waitress' tight jeans and a guy checking out a thong bikini on the beach. In both occasions the sunglasses come in handy. The guy can study the other chick all he wants and his girlfriend or wife never knows and still loves him at the end of the day.

If advertisers are now selling sunglasses based on the fact that men are secretly checking out women in front of their girlfriends, it's not hard to imagine what men are doing and not telling anyone about.

Two different worlds.

My wife and I caught a rerun of the British comedy **Coupling**. While we were watching and listening to the discussion of the three main characters who had just found a hot girl in a bar, my wife looked over at me and said, "men are pigs."

I didn't argue with her. The world he lives in and the world she lives in are not the same, and the one he lives in is much worse.

From the show ...

> Jeff: Do you know what would be the best way to wipe out all of human kind if you were a space alien with a special kind of mind ray ... Make all women telepathic. Because if they suddenly found out about the kind of stuff that goes on in our heads they would kill us all on the spot. Men are not people – we are disgustoids in human form.

Steve: When you say things like "nudity buffer," you actually expect people to know what you mean?

Jeff: Alright, when you first see a woman you like you have a buffer of about five minutes before you have fully mapped out what she looks like naked.

Patrick: A full five?

Jeff: You have to assess her nipple type and that takes time.

Patrick: Oh yeah, good point …

Patrick: Forget the nudity buffer. She just did another glance.

Jeff: Forget it? Forget the power of the buffer, Patrick? Did I ever tell you about the little redhead in my office?

Patrick: Never mind about the little redhead …

Jeff: Been there two years but I missed the buffer. That redhead has been naked in my head for two years now, performing deviant sex acts that would make the world's top porn stars go white and steady themselves on the furniture. I lose the ability to speak the moment she comes into the room. Every time she passes me in a corridor, I walk sideways into the wall. She thinks I'm a mute with a balance problem.[14]

Looking back at Adam and Eve in their little garden, I get a little envious. I wish I was in a spot where it was just me and my wife and no one else to distract us: no signs, billboards, tight shirts, low-cut pants, videos, songs, and everything else.

I can't help but wonder how that nasty smelling smoke changes me. I wonder if Adam would have cared anyway. He was consumed with Eve and nothing else. He knew she was him and he was her. Nothing else mattered in regards to other women.

He only had eyes for her.

Can I have that too?

There is a great scene in the movie *The Fellowship of the Ring*. Sam (a hobbit) is in love with a hobbit named Rosie. Sam is a nice hobbit and too shy to ever tell Rosie how he feels about her. As Sam is drinking a beer with his friend Frodo, Rosie is being hit on by a drunk hobbit. Sam starts to get a little worried.

Frodo tries to comfort him with this line:

> Don't worry, Sam,
> Rosie knows an idiot when she sees one.[15]

Here is my fear: it might work for hobbits but it doesn't seem to be working for us.

There are a lot of men who are drunk on self-fulfilling prophecies, using romance and love for their own benefit and, in short, living in a very different world than the women they are using.

Do women know an idiot when they see one?

Are they resisting before it's too late?

Do men know an idiot when they are one?

Are they resisting before it's too late?

Do you know an idiot? Are you resisting?

I suppose mediocrity knows.

I have built my organization upon fear.

Al Capone

five. fight.

Humpbacks swim every year from Alaska to Hawaii. That's a 3,000 mile swim. While in Hawaii, they have babies and hang out in with the babies in the warm waters of the tropics before heading back to Alaska for the summer.

While in Hawaii, there are competitions to see which male will escort the female and her new baby back to Alaska. These competitions turn into some amazing fights and shows of strength between the males who are trying to earn that right. The lucky winner swims alongside the female and her new baby for the entire 3,000 miles back. Along with the escorting duties, that male becomes the primary candidate for mating with the female.

No one has ever seen or recorded humpback whales mating, so no one really knows when or where or how they mate. Some say they mate in Hawaii, after the trip from Alaska, some say they mate in Alaska and some say they mate somewhere in-between, in the dark depths of the ocean.[1]

In the end, we know this: The males fight other males constantly, sometimes to the death, for the opportunity to swim 3,000 miles with a female and the opportunity to be the prime candidate for mating, if she decides.

Sometimes she picks another male.

In talking about the Bird of Paradise I said humans weren't too different from animals. Sometimes I wish we were more like animals, especially if those animals are Humpback whales.

For starters, whales never let anyone see them mate. Imagine what that would mean for humans for a moment.

Secondly, males fight with other males for a 3,000-mile trek with a female in order to prove their love and, maybe, have sex with her. It all

61

depends on whether she finds the male worthy or not – she never feels obligated.

In fact, once you start looking at the animal kingdom, you wonder who the more evolved species is. Females are often much smarter than we give them credit for in the animal kingdom when it comes to choosing partners.[2] Sometimes smarter than us humans.

Thirdly, though, we can learn from these whales, and most animals, that males need a good fight.

Remember Braveheart? Remember when Mel Gibson painted his face blue and came running down the hillside in his kilt with hundreds of guys behind him? He screams out for "Freedom!" and his mates run and yell and run and yell some more and men get chills because we see them amped up about fighting for something. We see them with a cause.

The author John Eldredge writes:

> In the heart of every man is a desperate desire for a battle to fight, an adventure to live, and a beauty to rescue.[3]

I would say that we're all fighting.

I would say that mediocrity knows this.

I would say that mediocrity has somehow, through the lies, gotten us to start fighting for him, instead of viewing him as the enemy to fight.

better
There are a wide range of numbers, but if you look up talking statistics, most of them say that women speak more words per day than men: 7,000 to 20,000 or something close to that.[4] There is other research that says women not only speak more words every day but also speak more words per minute than men. They are faster talkers.

So, all the jokes about trying to leave the party and the woman who "won't stop talking" are created …

fight

While I was writing this book, a new study came out that determined men use just about the same number of words as women.[5] (Is it just me or do scientific studies always determine something another scientific survey said wrong?)

Whether we can trust any of these studies, I don't know, but the study that says we all talk the same amount seems the accurate one to me. It always seemed like women could express themselves more clearly and eloquently than men, especially in regard to feelings, but it also seemed that men could keep up in the word count category as long as it was the right kind of talk.

If a man is interested, he can talk as well as any woman. If the conversation is sports, cars, movies, fishing, hunting, or whatever else pushes his button, he'll fly past 7,000 words without breaking a sweat.

Men also like to talk about women.

Bring up the topic of favorite celebrities, sexiest actresses, famous women you'd want to have sex with, and the talking starts ...

I have some buddies who, during their college days, would gather on a weekly basis in their frat house to listen to and give recaps of the week's dates with all the frat brothers in attendance.

> Wait until the boys hear about this one.

The more you look at men, the more you realize that this is a common occurrence.

> You should have seen the rack on this girl.

> Her? No way.

> I had that thing off before she could say anything. And she loved every minute of it.

So we fight. Not for a woman's respect, but for another man's.

The point of these recaps ...

THE NAKED FRUIT

is rarely to express how in love he is with her but to express how he used her to prove how much better he is to him.

We are competitive beings, us humans. We all want to prove we're better than the next person. If that means that a man needs to prove that he is better with women than his friend, and there is a woman around who can help him prove it, so be it.

Women, of course, are competitive as well, which works perfectly.

> If you have had sex with eight girls, three of whom were virgins, well you have definitely proven something to the guy still trying to get up his girlfriend's shirt.

> If you are the guy who walks around parties telling other guys to smell your fingers or your cheek you have definitely proven something to the guy still learning how to unclip a bra.

> If you are a girl who has had sex in a car, in your boyfriend's room, and in his basement while his parents were upstairs, well you have definitely proven something to the girl who has never even seen her boyfriend naked.

> If you are a girl who got another pearl necklace last night, and has a cell phone picture to prove it, well you have definitely proven something to the girl who doesn't even know what a pearl necklace is.

So all of us are trying to be better than each other and using the opposite sex to do it. Is this working for anyone?

What are we proving?

Maybe, that whales are smarter than us.

look
When I was a freshman in college I was hanging in my friend's dorm room one night. I had never met his roommate but he came in. We

talked for a few minutes and before I knew it, he was showing me a picture of his girlfriend naked, with her legs spread out.

I really wasn't sure what I was supposed to say to a guy who I didn't really know, showing me a picture of his girlfriend's fruits, and it was a little awkward. I just tilted my head to signify that he had proven something.

A friend of mine told me about running into a friend from High School who, five minutes into their reuniting conversation, pulled out a picture of his latest girlfriend so my friend could "check out her rack".

Of guys who receive nude cell phone pictures, 17% forward them on.[6] I don't think anyone sees the trends heading toward a decrease either.

Is this fight benefiting anyone besides mediocrity?

cherries

In Jr. High my English teacher had us students bring in songs every week and we would, as a class, go over the lyrics of the song. Of course Jr. High students are going to bring in stuff that they think their English teacher will flip over and that's exactly what we did. But, she never flipped, and it was kind of discouraging. She really was a good teacher.

I learned in that class what "bust a cherry" meant. Our teacher calmly informed us that to "bust a cherry" meant to have sex with a virgin.

Many years later I heard this story: Two brothers who were still in high school were hanging out with their older brother (out of high school) who was going through his old yearbook. He was pointing out to his little brothers all the "cherries he had busted": all the virgins he had been the first for.

I'm sure his little brothers were impressed.

If there was ever anything that didn't make a lot of sense to me, it's this: Why do guys brag about having sex with a virgin. Virgin sex is rarely synonymous with hot sex.

Right? And yet …

THE NAKED FRUIT

Virginity has long been a prized possession. Read anything about most cultures and you'll find virgins valued and women despised and ruined if they lost their virginity.

In ancient Athens women who lost their virginity before marriage were sold into slavery because they had no further worth and had ruined their family's name and reputation. Roman law once gave a father permission to kill his daughter and the man she had sex with if his daughter had lost her virginity before marriage.[7] The examples go on and on.

In India today, two-thirds of all men expect to marry a virgin. The problem is that half of them have been with a prostitute.[8] That statistic indicates all sorts of things including hypocrisy and a failure to see participation with a prostitute as connected in any way to marrying a virgin: a failure to see the system.

But it also indicates that men still have a desire for virgins.

Why?

Have you heard of hymenoplasty? It's a surgery to give a woman a new hymen so that the woman, and her partner, can experience virginity and the subsequent "deflowering" all over again.[9] Ignoring the fact that virginity is so much more than a piece of skin, the fact that women are paying thousands of dollars to have such surgeries for their boyfriends and/or husbands is indicative, again, of the desire of men for virginity (or one small aspect of virginity).

There was a woman in the news who was offering her virginity to the highest bidder. At the time of writing this over 10,000 men have offered money, and the bid is at $3.8 million.[10] If we need more proof that men value virginity, look no further than $3.8 million worth.

So what is it about the guy telling his little brothers about the cherries he had busted?

Was it good sex? What is hot sex?

I doubt it. But, it was, at least, proof virginity still matters in big ways.

fight

To this guy it was a way to prove to his little brothers that he was able to get something no other man had or ever will from that girl. To Indian men, it represents getting something no other man has had or ever will.

We're all the same.

Getting something no other person has ever had or ever will carries value: either to prove something to someone, or to appreciate something.

Who doesn't want the untouched treasure? Who doesn't want someone entirely and wholly yours that no one else has ever touched?

Who doesn't want what virginity represents: physical self-restraint, confidence, and power?

Who doesn't want to hear this?

> Out of six billion people on the planet, I choose you. And no one else. No one else gets this. No one else gets me in this specific, holy, sacred, emotional, spiritual, physical way.[11]

If we want it, why do we continue to ruin it, destroy it and take it?

Just to prove something to someone?

watch
Some friends of mine were at a high-school party back in the day and one of their friends told them that he was going to have sex with his sophomore girlfriend in the back room. The senior told his friends to go outside and look into the window.

So, my friends got some beer and moved outside of the house to the window. They didn't really think he was going to do it but they were having a good time anyway. Sure enough, the blinds on the window soon opened and their friend was doing his girlfriend doggie-style. He gave them the thumbs up to his buddies outside the window while the girl was looking down toward the bed with no idea she was being watched.

Maybe she loved the sex and maybe she loved the guy but I doubt she loved being the butt of a joke.

No one likes to be used. But when words, and photos, aren't enough, if you really want to prove something, just let them see it live-action.

get her
There is something inherently wrong with the words. Think about them for a second.

If she wants to, you don't have to get her to.

Where is
>earn
>justify
>and prove?

It's just get.

>Coerce
>convince
>and persuade.

I once read the theory that if you get a girl to come to your house and get her to take off her shoes in your house, you are more likely to get her to have sex with you because a girl, in this guy's opinion, was more likely to stay overnight after taking off her shoes because she was comfortable in the house.[12]

True or not, this kind of language is everywhere. Get her to do A and B and you will get her to do C in return.

Get her brings us back to the story of the garden doesn't it?

The whole thing was *getting* her to eat the fruit. Just g*et* her to look at it and convince her that it looks pretty tasty.

If we have to get someone to do something, it doesn't seem like it's usually for a very good reason.

>Get her to let you up her shirt.

fight

>Get her to give you a blow job.

>Get her to take off her panties.

Google has an auto-complete feature which means you can start to type in a search and Google will fill in the search with the most popular, similar searches.

If you type "How can I get my boyfriend to … "

Google will give you

>propose.
>spend more time with me.

If you type "How can I get my girlfriend to … "

Google will give you

>give me head.
>sleep with me.[13]

Did Adam ever have to *get* Eve to do anything?

I wonder if in getting each other to do this and that …

Mediocrity is getting us …

boss
We are fighting. We are proving. We are earning.

For what?

It seems we are fighting for short term thrills, for mediocrity, for bad fruit in a world where good, delightful, joyful, and beautiful still exist.

Why?

Because it's fun. We can at least admit that.

It's fun working for the powerful dictator or bad ass crime boss. We've all seen the movies. The boss gives us cars, clothes, houses, women, guns, and everything else we could ask for.

Most importantly, he gives us a sense of power.

It's fun to be that guy's henchman. It's fun to be his servant. It's powerful to take out the people he doesn't like, to torture those who go against him, to burn down the houses of those who don't believe in him. It's fun to represent him, to feel the fear of those who look at us and say, "He works for … "

It's fun to feed our ego. It feels good.

So we brag. I mentioned the Iraqi women earlier. There are entire websites dedicated to men bragging about their escapades with prostitutes, not just in Iraq, but all around the world. Country after country, city after city, and forum post after forum post.[14]

It strikes me as so strange. What is there to brag about when you paid a woman to do it?

But that doesn't matter. It's not the fact that they got something from a woman. It's the fact that other men will listen to what they got and be impressed with it. It's the power. It's the bravado of who is in charge.

From the sorority girl across Greek Row to the teenage prostitutes of Asia, men can't wait to tell someone the whole story because it brings them power and power feels good, every time, even if it comes from fighting for the wrong guy.

At least in the short term.

The danger is, however, in the long term. Does it pay off?

Are we are becoming powerful or enslaved?

Are *we* advancing or is mediocrity?

It seems that as mediocrity gains power, we lose power.

There always comes a point in working for the enemy that we start to

fight

ask the questions ...

> If my boss is so powerful, so rich, and so intimidating, why does he need me?
>
> If my boss sends me on missions of destruction so nonchalantly, what will he care about sending someone on the mission to destroy me?
>
> What if I don't want to carry out an order someday?
>
> What if I ever want to leave?
>
> What if none of this is for my benefit and all of it is for his?

Erwin Rommel was one of Hitler's prized field marshals. He fought in the northern deserts of Africa commanding a Panzer tank division. He fought for a master of lies, eventually getting most of an entire nation to believe his lies. Rommel dedicated his life to reducing Hitler's foes to dirt and he did a fantastic job.

Rommel fought for the man who said to make the lie big, make it simple, and keep repeating it.

Rommel's life ended with these words to his son:

> I have just had to tell your mother, that I shall be dead in a quarter of an hour ... To die by the hand of one's own people is hard. But the house is surrounded and Hitler is charging me with high treason ... I am to have the chance of dying by poison. The two generals have brought it with them. It's fatal in three seconds. If I accept, none of the usual steps will be taken against my family, that is against you. They will also leave my staff alone.[15]

Rommel fought a long time for something he believed in. He dedicated his life, his family, his studies, his whole self to that master. It felt right and it felt good. It felt as though he was doing something that would benefit him.

Until it didn't.

By then the master he was fighting for turned around and killed him without hesitating. Rommel didn't realize he was fighting for the wrong guy until it was too late.

We rarely do.
If you believe the statistics that Americans rate their sex life at a 6.5 out of 10[16], I'm not sure our current way of doing things is really benefiting us that much.

In fact, I'd say 6.5 out of 10 is pretty mediocre.

And, somehow, we keep fighting for more mediocrity?

>It's one thing to lie to ourselves.
>It's another thing to believe it.[17]

fight

The ego wants to find a way to avoid changing if at all possible.

Richard Rohr

Our efforts to thwart the law of natural consequences merely make the penalty more crushing when it comes.

J. Budziszewski, The Revenge of Conscience

six. boomerang.

They were naked.
It was …
    Beautiful.
    Delightful.
    Joyful.
    Precious.
    Good.

There were some lies about fruit.
The good gave way to things that are not good because the naked people ate the fruit.
There is still …
    Beautiful.
    Delightful.
    Joyful.
    Precious.
    Good.

There is still fruit and there are lies about it.
Mediocrity is growing and mediocrity is not …
    Beautiful.
    Delightful.
    Joyful.
    Precious.
    Good.

Nor does mediocrity like them.
We're fighting for more mediocrity
    when we just want to be naked and good again.

If you remember nothing else in this entire book, remember this:

    Our actions
    however harmless they appear on the surface
    are coming back to haunt us and destroy
    beautiful, delightful, joyful, precious, and good.

THE NAKED FRUIT

Don't throw a boomerang if you don't want to catch it later.

Maybe you don't agree. Maybe you're not convinced our actions are harming anything. Maybe you're not convinced of the system.

You need to be convinced. I'm convinced it's foundational to why we're so far away from where we started.

[This chapter is not a pretty one. It's direct and blunt. Our world can be very ugly, which makes this chapter an ugly one. I happen to think this might be the most important chapter in the book but I also understand that there are some people in this world who would be more harmed than helped by reading this chapter. If you think you might be one of those people, at least tread lightly. Skip it altogether if you feel you should.][1]

It started out beautiful. We can all find things that are a long way from beautiful.

The question is, do we think we are contributing? Are we, in our fight for mediocrity, contributing to a world where the short term outweighs the long?

Are we contributing to a world that believes consequences don't exist, or at least keeps them hidden?

The consequences I'm talking about aren't things like sexually transmitted diseases and pregnancy. Those are far too easy and obvious.

Mediocrity isn't that stupid.

mediocrity genius
In fact, I'm convinced that getting us to focus on STD's and pregnancy is just another one of mediocrity's plans. He's sneaky like that. Think about what the focus does.

For starters, looking at porn and going to strip clubs are out. Neither of them cause STD's nor gets anyone pregnant. If the consequences are STD's and pregnancy, definitely no problems with porn and strip clubs.

boomerang

In addition, while one out of four American teenage girls has an STD[2], three out of four don't.

Most people don't get STD's.

While there are thousands of unwanted pregnancies among teenagers every year, there are millions of teenagers having sex, not resulting in unwanted pregnancies.

The fact is that most people don't get pregnant when they don't want to.

Maybe all those great marketing campaigns and high school assemblies are playing right into the hands of mediocrity.

What happens when we focus on consequences that don't happen to everyone? If most people don't experience the consequences than it's pretty easy to convince ourselves that the short-term thrill is worth it.

If STD's and unwanted pregnancies are the long term consequences that we're talking about, then the short-term thrill is worth it for most people.

There are few things that mediocrity would rather have us thinking.

I sometimes wonder if he laughs at logic like that.

There was a poll in the UK that asked kids what they thought was the very best thing in the world. The first-place answer was "being a celebrity." Second was "being rich" and third "good looks."[3]

If being a celebrity is the best thing in the world, what will we do to get it? Steven Pressfield, in *The War of Art* has a suggestion:

> Why put in years of work designing a new software interface when you can get just as much attention by bringing home a boyfriend with a prison record?[4]

Dramatic?

A Girls Gone Wild rep was being interviewed on a television show. She said women line up, begging to be on their show. They'll lift their shirts, make out with other girls, or whatever else, to "be famous."

Mediocrity probably smiles.

I just saw an ad for some cologne with the tag line "Only (this cologne) could make pretty young ladies forget their intimate clothes in men's bathrooms."[5] The ad campaign places images of bras and panties in men's bathrooms in different clubs and restaurants.

There was another ad by the same company, this time for a series of body washes.[6] The first wash is to "get caliente", the second is in case you "can't remember the night before", the third is to "wake the f--- up" and the fourth is to "scrub away the skank".

Skank generally refers to a young girl who is "easy."

So four body washes to help you hook up with an easy girl and then forget about her.

In doing "research" for this book I've read quite a few dating books that are out there, many of which I reference at some point or another in this book.[7] Here's a summary of things women are supposed to do to make men attracted to them.

> Make the bed after you spend the night with him.
> Cook for him.
> Wear lingerie.
> Walk to the fridge naked.
> Bend over at the waist.
> Don't spend the night the first few times since men need their alone bubble.
> Be happy and peppy around him.
> Look at porn for shaving tips.
> Have sex with him the first time in his bed because your bed is sacred.
> Say "tits" and "ass."

And on and on the list goes.

Is this funny?

boomerang

Are these choices, these voices, these lies and these distortions doing anything to damage the system we all live in?

Are they already coming back to haunt us?

Maybe you need convincing. Maybe we need an illustration.

Let's take the idea that men *need* to go to strip clubs, since we've already talked a little about it.

At first glance, it's fun. There are some short-term thrills and almost no long-term consequences for us or anyone else. There are no STD's and no unwanted pregnancies and probably a horny man for his girlfriend/wife.

Right?

So John decides he should go. John craves a naked woman and needs variety and for a few bucks he can satisfy both.

No harm, no foul.

Right off the bat, John helps the industry make billions of dollars. Women hear about billions of dollars and wonder why men like John have to go. John leads to his own girlfriend wondering why she isn't good enough for John. John makes other women wonder why they aren't hot enough for their boyfriends or men in general because men spend a lot of money on seeing other women.

John has contributed to making women become conscious about their weight, their body, and their sex appeal. John has contributed to women who look at celebrities who have "no problem" with sex appeal. John had encouraged women to want to be like those women and thus copy their lifestyles, or better, their perceived lifestyles.

John has just contributed to bulimia, anorexia, and a plethora of other crap, including women who probably don't feel comfortable in front of their own husbands and now don't have sex as much (contributing to the penny jar problem) as well as women who feel so far from confident that they are desperate for approval from men (contributing to a host of other problems).

Of course, he's only contributed a drop in the ocean. He's hardly done a thing.

Unfortunately, there are millions of John and oceans are just lots of drops that don't think they've done a thing.

If you've never read C.S. Lewis' *The Screwtape Letters*, you really should. The book is a series of letters written between two demons, talking about the lies they are telling humanity and the best ways to screw the humans over. At one point, in a letter to a demon he is mentoring, the senior demon Screwtape says this to his young apprentice:

> As a result, we are more and more directing the desires of men to something which does not exist – making the role of the eye in sexuality more and more important and at the same time making its demands more and more impossible. What follows you can easily forecast![8]

Can we forecast what the strip club does?

Are we already at a point where the demands are almost impossible?

Can women meet the demands? How hard will they try? How far will a man go to get a woman who he thinks does? Will she?

I mentioned Girls Gone Wild, which makes billions of dollars filming college girls lifting their shirts, making out with each other, and grinding on guys, most often on Spring Break vacations.

Here is a story about Joe Francis, the founder of Girls Gone Wild, taken from the LA Times. Szyszka is a woman Joe Francis met in a club. She recounts her story.

> Szyszka tells me later that as she was spinning around the strip pole that night, Francis appeared, grabbed her arm and pulled her toward him. "You are so going on the bus later," she recalls Francis saying. "I was like, 'Um, OK.' I was shocked. I was like, 'Whoa—Joe's, like, trying to talk to me, like out of all the girls in here.'" Francis invited her back to the VIP area to do shots with him, she says, and she said yes.

Szyszka says the more shots she drank, the cloudier her judgment became. She says she agreed to join Francis and his crew on the "Girls Gone Wild" bus. "I thought 'Girls Gone Wild' was like flashing, and I thought I would flash them and be done. And so when I'm walking to the bus, that's all I'm thinking is going to happen."

At first she felt comfortable, she says. Inebriated and excited, she says she was led to the back of the bus, to a small bedroom. The double bed, with its neatly folded iridescent purple sheets, takes up most of the room. A flat-screen TV faces the bed, and cabinets are filled with remote controls, lubricants, condoms, sex toys in plastic bags, baby oil, a DVD called "How to be a Player" and a clipboard full of waivers for girls to sign. A small bathroom is off to the side, with a half-sized shower with faux marble tiling, and on the floor of the shower is a crate holding cheap and fruity-flavored rum, whiskey, tequila and Kool-Aid.

Footage from that night shows a close-up of Szyszka's driver's license, proving she's not a minor. The camera then captures Szyszka lying on the bed. Her nails are chipped, her eyes coated with makeup. Following a cameraman's instructions, she shows her breasts and says, "Girls Gone Wild." She seems shy but willing. She smiles. The unseen cameraman asks her to take off her shirt, her skirt, then her underwear. She sprawls on the bed, her legs open. At his suggestion, she masturbates with a dildo, saying repeatedly that it hurts but also feels good. Francis enters the room at certain points and you hear his voice, low and flirtatious, telling her, "You are so adorable." When she says she's a virgin, he responds: "Great. You won't be after my cameraman gets done with you."

When I talk to Szyszka seven days later, she says she "didn't quite realize" she was being filmed. "But I didn't care because I was drunk and who cares?" Then she adds: "It didn't feel good to me at all, but I was totally faking it because I was on 'Girls Gone Wild.' "

Eventually, Szyszka says, Francis told the cameraman to leave and pushed her back on the bed, undid his jeans and climbed on top of her. "I told him it hurt, and he kept doing it. And I keep telling him it hurts. I said, 'No' twice in the beginning, and during I started saying, 'Oh, my god, it hurts.' I kept telling him it hurt, but he kept going, and he said he was sorry but kissed me so I wouldn't keep talking."

Afterward, she says, Francis cleaned them both off with a paper towel and told her to get dressed. Then, she says, he opened the door and told the cameraman to come back, saying, "She's not a virgin anymore."[9]

Strip clubs. Minimize the distance from drinking to sex. Celebrity. Virginity. A carton of cigarettes. Fighting for mediocrity. Meeting the demands.

When it all comes together at once, it's not pretty.

In fact, it's very ugly.

She brought it on herself, we argue. She was stupid. She shouldn't have been there in the first place. It's always easy to blame. Of course, she should have some blame put on her.

But maybe there is a bigger question: What has my contribution been to the system she found herself in?

I ran across a blog whose author is a self-proclaimed sex fiend. She chronicles her "casual sex" encounters and claims to enjoy her sex life quite a bit.

The first time I saw her blog it read like this:

> It's not like I had any right to be upset by his leaving – this was casual sex, nothing more. But I really enjoyed his company: I wouldn't have f---d him so many times if I didn't. Partly this was because he was a fantastic

lover and our sexual chemistry seemed perfectly matched: the sex we had was amazing. But he was also rather different to other men I have been with: I had been taken aback by his cooking a three-course meal for me on our first date; his reading Philosophy in bed turned me on and made me want to jump him; the way he would meditate rather than just fall asleep after having sex, showed another, deeper, sensitivity to his masculinity that I found very attractive alongside his handsomeness.

And during the last six months where circumstances had made me feel needy and vulnerable, alongside being horny and craving sex, he became a sort of trusted solace for me: he was someone with whom I wouldn't have to keep up a façade. He didn't seem to judge me — he just accepted me for who I was — so as a result, I could lose myself in passion with him without worrying about any negative consequences – for either of us. I guess given all this, it was only natural for me to fancy him: I looked forward to seeing him when both our schedules allowed.

I had considered the romantic possibilities of course, but there were many reasons why we were not well matched to be a couple ...

Until he left me alone in the hotel room, I suppose I hadn't realised how much I might want something more with him and how disappointed I might be, if he didn't want that too. Faced with the hard reality — the abrupt impersonal peck on the cheek showing he didn't want to be intimate with me — I had to accept that this want was one-sided.

As I looked at my reflection in the mirror, I felt stupid. Stupid for letting my guard down; stupid for allowing myself to have even considered being more than f-buddies with him; and more stupid for feeling rejected by him, when there was absolutely nothing to feel rejected over.[10]

She felt stupid and rejected. How many more of us feel rejected and stupid, trying to meet the demands?

But there is more to John and his strip club experience. What about the women who strip? What do they have to say?

> I never prostituted myself but just having men say those things to you over and over each night takes a toll on you … You become real aware of men and their energy and when they're looking at you and if they're looking at you in a sexual way. I'm unable to relate intimately with not only just men on an emotional level but also with women and friends and family. When you're dancing, there is a wall that you have to put up between yourself and whoever you're entertaining and you have to learn how to put that wall up. You realize that nobody can get in after so long.
>
> But the big part of it is, after so long, operating like that, you realize that you can't get out, even when you want to. You don't even know how to connect as a normal, emotional, healthy human being.[11]

Has John ever wondered about the long-term consequences of the girl he is watching take off her clothes? If John doesn't think he's playing a part in those consequences, he might want to ask himself which one of the men who watches her is.

I would assume that none of the men would take the blame, which is exactly the way mediocrity likes it.

No blame, no shame.

Just a few more drops in an ugly ocean that continues to grow larger and larger.

From 2001 to 2005 there were 2,570 incidents of teachers being punished for sexual misconduct toward their students.[12]

There are 116,000 searches for child pornography every day.[13]

boomerang

The FBI estimates that well over 100,000 children and young women are trafficked as sex slaves in America. The average age of these sex slaves is 11.[14]

Here's a sample story:

> There were many women in this one apartment. Some were crying. Others looked terrified. We were told not to speak to each other. Not to tell each other our names or where we were from. All the time, very mean and ugly men came in and dragged girls into the rooms. Sometimes they would rape girls in front of us. They yelled at them, ordering them to move certain ways ... to pretend excitement ... to moan ... It was sickening. Those who resisted were beaten. If they did not cooperate, they were locked in dark cellars with rats with no food or water for three days. One girl refused to submit to anal sex, and that night the owner brought in five men. They held her on the floor and every one of them had anal sex on her in front of us all. She screamed and screamed, and we all cried. That girl killed herself the next day.[15]

One in four girls and one in six boys are sexually abused by the age of 18. Those numbers lead to 39 million people who are survivors of sexual abuse living in America today.[16]

MySpace has revealed they removed 90,000 sex offenders from their site over a two year period.[17]

How and where does the desire for such a thing originate?

Does John and his need to see strippers play any part in any of that desire, in any of these stories and statistics?

What about if John takes a look at some pornography every now and then?

Every second, $3,075.64 is spent on pornography.[18]

A lot of people are apparently taking some looks every now and then.

Do we think about the women who we are looking at? Jersey Jaxin starred in numerous pornos and said this:

> I never thought that I would be going home bleeding from being ripped, or bruised, or having welts and cuts from them whipping me and tying me up ... so I finally had it and had to get out of there because it drove me to pieces ... They take it further and further every single time to where when it comes to, the end, they don't care ... if you're limping out of there ... they don't care as long as they got their footage and you didn't mess up ... You get paid the same whether you're being tied up and whipped and you're getting ripped to pieces and bleeding and bruised or if you're doing just something what they call soft-core – to where it's simulated love-making. You get paid the same check every time ... You go home, you lay in your bed, you cry, you wondering what the hell am I doing to myself? ... Sometimes you don't even get your pay ... You can't exactly call your mom and say this is my problem. How do you expect your mom to understand that you just had sex with three guys and, guess what, you didn't get a paycheck? ... You just have to hold it all inside of you and it rips you apart and you break down, and you mentally, physically, and emotionally, want to die.[19]

Here is the experience of another porn star, named Ballowe, taken from another LA Times article:

> Legal and medical records show she walked away from the business in 1998 with chlamydia, which could make her sterile; cytomegalovirus, which could eventually make her blind; hepatitis C, which has damaged her liver; and HIV, which could cause AIDS and probably kill her. According to medical records, her liver is too damaged – in part because of the hepatitis – to allow her to take the anti-viral drugs that could delay the onset of AIDS ... Along the way, she also became a drug addict, and she has exhibited symptoms of schizophrenia ... staring at the TV screen inside a friend's apartment, Ballowe watches a clip from a 1998 video she made

> ... It is the film in which Ballowe has alleged she was infected with HIV ... She was paid $10,000 for her work, but records show the check bounced just days after she learned that she was HIV positive.
>
> As the video plays, Ballowe quietly excuses herself and walks into the bathroom, locking the door behind her. Water runs into the sink, nearly muffling the sound of retching.[20]

Of course watching those women can get addicting. Here is a line from a 22-year-old guy who became addicted to watching girls like Jersey and Ballowe:

> It wasn't just girls on a web page anymore, or girls on a TV. It was girls that walked down a hallway. It was my friends ... who I was looking at in such a disgusting, demeaning way. It's hard for me now even to have a normal, a respectful relationship with a girl.[21]

These are the big stories, the ones that make the papers.

What part does John play in these stories? What part do I play in these stories?

What part do I play in the smaller stories?

Go talk to people you know and you'll find the smaller stories. You'll meet plenty of real "statistics" who have experienced the "not so great" part of short-term thrills and lies.

You'll meet people who are imprisoned with comparisons between their wives and girls from the past. The thoughts of "why isn't she like her" drift across their minds and haunt them. They can't get rid of them even though they are madly in love with their wives. They beg for the images to leave but they never do.

You'll meet students who are under pressure to have sex, give a quick blow job to a "friend" after school, or students who regret that in their first sexual experiences, with ecstasy and a bunch of friends in a warehouse, things didn't go so well.

THE NAKED FRUIT

You'll meet women who now carry a STD because of a couple of nights in high school. Even though the odds are against it, 25% is a lot of women, and I wonder if the man who gave her the STD even remembers her name. I wonder if, while bragging about the number of girls he had sex with to prove something to another guy, he ever thinks of the consequences he'll never learn of.

Though the odds are against them, you'll meet couples who got pregnant and then married, and not because they wanted it in that order. We know plenty; some of them who are our good friends. Some of those stories turn out great. Some don't.

1.7 million babies were born in America in 2007 to moms that were not married.[22]

You'll meet men and women torn up with jealousy over past relationships.

You'll meet men who value virginity more than they let on, and who are messed up over the fact that she gave herself to someone other than him.

You'll meet people who leave their wives and children because they became addicted to looking at pictures of naked women on their computer. They choose the images over the family that they created.

You'll meet single moms raising teenagers, finding it hard to get married, because of a night in college.

You'll meet 75-year-old women who say this about a relationship that occurred over 50 years earlier. As she talks you'll see the hurt and damage on her face, even though she's lived a full life since then.

> I gave myself to him. I slept with him. I bore him children. I still can't understand how he could say he didn't love me any longer. I don't understand.

Mediocrity is sly. The lies are clever, otherwise we wouldn't believe them.

We need variety. We need porn. We need strip clubs. We need sex.

boomerang

It's all healthy.

Make the lie big, make it simple, keep saying it, and eventually they will believe it.

Anthony DeMello wrote this:

> That is what your mind can become – flabby, covered with layers of fat till it becomes too dull and lazy to think, to observe, to explore, to discover. It loses its alertness, its aliveness, its flexibility and goes to sleep.[23]

Have we become too dull and lazy to think, to observe, to explore, and to even discover …

Beautiful.
Delightful.
Joyful.
Precious.
Good.

I was drinking coffee with a friend when he told me this:

> I remember clearly my "first time." It was high school. Everyone was telling me that we had to do it. So, we finally decided that we should. First, it was in my old car. Not the best spot. Second, I don't remember how long it lasted, but it wasn't very long. I don't really remember the sex at all. I do remember her crying in my arms for four hours afterward. I felt horrible. Four hours. I still feel horrible.

Even the small stories are pretty big for the people who were there.

I think we all need to feel a little more sick at the stories like this. Sometimes the sick feelings get through the flabby layers of fat in our mind that the lies have created.

What part does John play?

What part do you play?

What part do I play?

The great Russian writer Dostoevsky:

> Those outbursts of cruel sensuality which overtake almost everybody on our earth, whether man or woman, and are the only source of almost every sin of our human race.[24]

Cruel sensuality. It's a system wide problem now.

The lies are clever.

The British writer J.G. Ballard:

> A widespread taste for pornography means that nature is alerting us to some threat of extinction.[25]

70% of men between 18 to 24 years old visit porn sites in a typical month. 40% of Americans are regular visitors to porn sites.[26]

Widespread.

David Mura said it this way:

> Those in the thrall of pornography try to eliminate from their consciousness the world outside pornography, and this includes everything from their family and friends or last Sunday's sermon to the political situation in the Middle East. In engaging in such elimination the viewer reduces himself. He becomes stupid.[27]

The source of almost every sin.

> An alert to the threat of extinction.

> Stupid.

I don't think we need more stories, statistics, and quotes.

boomerang

I hope not.

But, we have to get it. We have to understand what we're doing.

All of us.

Our world is filled with the effects of John, of me and you: from friends I have coffee with to sex slaves forced to have anal sex. It's ugly. It's wrong. And it's tearing our world apart from the seams.

It's far worse than we pretend it is.

But, it's not what this book is about. It's about

> Beautiful.
>
> Delightful.
>
> Joyful.
>
> Precious.
>
> Good.

And getting back there.

I hope we all realize we're traveling farther away every moment.

More importantly, I hope we all realize the story isn't over.

Him and her. Me and you.

We're all here. Our stories are not finished.

We've moved the wrong way. Maybe we didn't realize how far. But we can still move back toward something beautiful, delightful, joyful, precious, and good.

Does anyone want to?

*All truths are easy to understand once they are discovered;
the point is to discover them.*

Galileo Galilei

seven. love is fruit.

I was talking to a friend about definitions: about words and their meanings. Our communication, obviously, depends on them.

Good.

    We all know what it means right?

    But why are some things good to some people and not to others?

        The war in Iraq.
        Pornography.
        The movie *Avatar*.

    Do we really agree on what good means?

Rape.

We can look up the definition

    to force someone to have sex without their consent or against their will.

Consent?

The radio host Tom Leykis says this:

    Regardless of the situation, when a woman says no, stop whatever you are doing or about to do and get out. Even if you are in the middle of hot steamy sex and she says no, you stop what you're doing and get out.

    No does not mean she is playing.
    No does not mean just this one time.
    No does not mean she consents to sex.

But earlier I quote Tom Leykis as saying that you should never compliment a woman because that raises her self-esteem and will lessen your chances of having sex.

Obviously, it would lessen her chances of saying no. Is that really the heart of consent?

What about "against their will"?

Does a girl who has sex because she was too shy to say no, or too afraid to say no, or talked into it by her boyfriend count?

Get her. When is that against her will?

Definitions are problematic. Especially if we're going to move back toward the words we're trying to move back toward, like beauty, delight, joy, precious and good.

There is a key word in this whole journey and we've already mentioned it.

Love.

We know we all need it, but what do we need?

I love a book.
I love a beer.
I love a movie.
I love sex.
I love a girl.
I love my nephew.
I love my wife.
I love my daughter.
I love spaghetti.

Was the Hollywood star who stayed married 9 months just as in love with his spouse as Marlow and Frances Cowan who played the piano together at the Mayo Clinic?

Is love really that sporadic and random?

love is fruit

Can we move back toward beauty, delight, joy, precious, and good without being on the same page in regards to love?

I don't think so.

In the Greek language (and others) there are four words to describe love because there are four varieties of love. Science agrees, saying that these varieties of love are "fueled by a differing set of chemicals and hormones, and each runs through a disparate neuronal circuit."[1]

So let's look at the four Greek categories[2] so we can say

>I love you

>and

>I love you too

>and mean the same thing.

eros

Eros is the first of the words and the first category of love. Eros is the word that most men would use for love if we had four words for love in English (and if men weren't intentionally lying). It's where English gets the word for erotica: we're talking about sex, nudity, and the stuff that is related to sex and nudity. More technically, it means passion or romantic love.

Eros is the scene where shirts are flying through the air hitting the ceiling fan, feet are hitting wine glasses and spilling Syrah onto the carpet, and two people are jumping onto a kitchen table in a frenetic scene of unquenchable sexual energy.

This is the picture men often think about when they think of "love" in regards to a woman.

When a man says he loves a woman, especially early on in a relationship, what he really means is I eros you. In other words,

>I love the passionate feelings I get inside me and I love imagining you naked and I love the fact that someday,

THE NAKED FRUIT

maybe sooner than later, I'm not going to have to imagine anymore and we're going to 'get it on' while our clothes twirl on the ceiling fan above us.

I eros you.

Eros is amazing but in the way that a salad dressing is amazing. Very few people eat dressing by itself. A dressing has no real nutritional value and frankly isn't very good if that's all you're eating

But dressing makes a lot of other foods, that actually have nutritional value, taste so good. Carrots, lettuce, chicken wings, and on and on it goes …

That's eros. A dressing for the other loves …

philia
Philia means friendship. It is the love of friends.

It is the reason girls will tell each other "I love you" about ten times as much as guys do.

When guys say, "I love you," they are most often thinking eros and the majority of men don't want to tell another guy that they want to have sex with them.

So, instead of saying, "I love you" guys say, "you're a stud" and "what's up, dog?" and other things that mean, "You're my friend and I've got strong friend feelings for you but they are not sexual in any way."

I philia you.

When girls say, "I love you" they are often thinking philia, and so they say, "I love you" all the time to each other. I love being your friend.

With these two words, we quickly discover why definitions are so important.

"I love you babe." "I love you too."

love is fruit

The girl in the relationship is thinking,

> "That is so cool that he wants to build a deep friendship."

And the guy in the relationship is thinking,

> "That is so cool that she wants to get naked."

That conversation is ripe for trouble.

> Don't you care about me?
>
> What, you don't want to have sex with me?
>
> I thought you *loved* me!
>
> I thought *you* loved me!

All of this brings up the question of whether guys want to, or can be, friends with girls at all.

It's an old movie, but "When Harry Met Sally" gave an answer:

> Harry: You realize of course that we could never be friends.
>
> Sally: Why not?
>
> Harry: What I'm saying is — and this is not a come-on in any way, shape or form — is that men and women can't be friends because the sex part always gets in the way.
>
> Sally: That's not true. I have a number of men friends and there is no sex involved.
>
> Harry: No you don't.
>
> Sally: Yes I do.

THE NAKED FRUIT

Harry: No you don't.

Sally: Yes I do.

Harry: You only think you do.

Sally: You say I'm having sex with these men without my knowledge?

Harry: No, what I'm saying is they all WANT to have sex with you.

Sally: They do not.

Harry: Do too.

Sally: They do not.

Harry: Do too.

Sally: How do you know?

Harry: Because no man can be friends with a woman that he finds attractive. He always wants to have sex with her.

Sally: So, you're saying that a man can be friends with a woman he finds unattractive?

Harry: No. You pretty much want to nail 'em too.

Sally: What if THEY don't want to have sex with YOU?

Harry: Doesn't matter because the sex thing is already out there so the friendship is ultimately doomed and that is the end of the story.

Sally: Well, I guess we're not going to be friends then.

Harry: I guess not.

love is fruit

> Sally: That's too bad. You were the only person I knew in New York.

Do men want to be friends with women? Yes. They do.

Sometimes because they want to have sex.
Sometimes because they want to break up a relationship.
Sometimes because they just like hanging out.
Sometimes because they can't imagine life without her.

Philia is like a carrot. It's pretty good to eat on its own.

However, throw in some dressing (maybe ranch or bleu cheese) with your carrot and yum … a best friend who you can have sex with?

storge
Before I go to bed, I head into my daughters' rooms and "tuck them in." There are nights when I pull up the covers over my sweet little 5-year-old and watch her snuggle with a smile on her face. I stare at her for about ten seconds. That is the third kind of love: storge.

In my opinion, storge is one of the most beautiful and moving loves: A mother staring into the face of her infant, a father playing baseball in a park, or two soon-to-be parents touching a pregnant belly. The images of children and newborns are often associated with it, because it's such a pure, clean love and kids express purity better than anything else.

There was an uproar over a piece of writing from a woman named Kate Moses. She wrote a book as well as a controversial article in the New York Times.

Her exact words, in one section talking about her daughter, go like this:

> I do love her. But I'm not in love with her. Nor with her two brothers or sisters. Yes, I have four children. Four children with whom I spend a good part of every day: bathing them, combing their hair, sitting with them while they do their homework, holding them while they weep their tragic tears. But I'm not in love with any of them. I am in love with my husband.[3]

There were a lot of people outraged over her comments. It was big conversation on daytime talk shows and chaos ensued from a simple statement saying she loved her husband differently than her children.

Not to speak for Moses, but I think she was trying to put thoughts into English that we're not used to expressing. I think she was saying that she feels an affection, a care, a nurturing for her children that is not like the feelings she has for her husband. Personally, I think that's a good thing.

She loves them both, but differently. She loves them both with the same amount of love but different forms of love.

Storge is also an amazing form of love. It's not erotic (which would be weird for kids) and it's not philia (I hope children are more than friends), but it's tender and endearing. It's innocent and lovely and beautiful.

While it's most often illustrated through children, it certainly doesn't lose anything when it's applied to lovers.

Twilight. You've heard of the series I'm sure. If not, the books (and movies) are a love story between a modern-day vampire, Edward, and a girl, Bella. My wife read the books and enjoyed them, but here's one of the main reasons why:

> With deliberate slowness, his hands slid down the sides of my neck. I shivered, and I heard him catch his breath. But his hands didn't pause as they softly moved to my shoulders, and then stopped.
>
> His face drifted to the side, his nose skimming across my collarbone. He came to rest with the side of his face pressed tenderly against my chest.
>
> Listening to my heart.[4]

We all need our faces touched, whether we admit it or not. We all need love and we need that love expressed through simple, nurturing affection. We need a clean touch, unassociated with an agenda of eros, pure and beautiful.

love is fruit

We need someone to listen to our hearts.

Storge is like a good salad. Clean, crisp lettuce that offers a full meal. If you like dressing, add a little to the top and the salad just gets that much better.

agape
A ...

Beautiful
Delightful
Joyful
Precious
and Good

Love.

This is the one.

Agape is what we all need and crave and desire.
Agape is a love that cannot be expressed nonchalantly.

Sure the salad with dressing and carrots is there and tastes good but it's just a part of the larger meal. Agape is the meal.

Agape is not limited to male/female sexual relationships but when it's there, it's ...

what we think we mean when we often don't.
what wives want their husbands to give them,
and husbands want their wives to give them.

Agape is the pinnacle, the zenith, the best of the best loves.

Agape is the one that we're substituting a lot of other loves for.

Agape is self-sacrificial.

Agape's concern is for the person receiving the love more than the person giving it.

Agape is the best of eros, philia, and storge combined into one all-encompassing, powerful, blow-your-mind love. It is the ultimate friendship combined with the ultimate eroticism, affection, innocence, and beauty, all wrapped up with commitment, honor, and dedication.

It is a love without conditions.

Yeah, agape is very good, very beautiful, very joyful, very precious and very delightful. It's filling.

Agape, however, does not come easy. That means it's hard. We live in a world where we like easy over hard. We'd rather swing through the drive-through and grab some eros on the way home instead of breaking out all the pots and pans to put together all of the ingredients into a homemade agape feast.

Agape does not break over "irreconcilable differences," because agape views "irreconcilable differences" as just another chance to prove devotion and allegiance. Eros might recoil at the differences, but agape will say bring it on.

many days
There is a story[5] that is thousands of years old and was meant to represent agape.

The story goes like this.

A man was told to marry a prostitute.

Most men do not want to marry prostitutes, and, I assume, this man was no different.

He was told to marry the prostitute and show her agape – to love her unconditionally.

So, he did. They got married and they had sex. She eventually had a son and a daughter with her husband. They were creating a happy little family, about to build the picket fence, but things went bad. The man's wife returned to her old ways and started sleeping around for money again.

love is fruit

Most men do not want to marry a prostitute, but they really, really don't want their wife to be a prostitute while they are married. I assume this man was no different.

But the man was told to take his wife back and continue to love her. The crazy thing is that he does. When he does, he says this to her:

> You are to live with me many days; you must not be a prostitute or be intimate with any man, and I will live with you.[6]

How about no more days?

Even after that line, his wife continues to disgrace his love.

Think about that. This man's wife is having sex with lots of other men while he takes care of her, supports her needs, and tries to love her. He says to her that she is to live with him many days. He cares for her, buys her clothes and food, while she continues to disgrace him by having sex with other men – and yet he continues to love her.

Are you kidding me?

Take your wife back after she has an affair and continue to be married after she carries out prostitution with other men? For many days? It's crazy, nuts, and absurd. For this man to continue to love that woman, goes against everything we are taught that love is.

But a love without conditions, a love that sacrifices, a love wrapped in honor, commitment, and dedication is that radical.

The story makes a powerful, almost unbelievable, point: nothing breaks agape.

Nothing.

Our culture is a bit in love with eros. In fact, we're eros for eros. We are infatuated with infatuation, hot and heavy for being hot and heavy and erotic for erotica.

Somehow we have convinced ourselves and actually believe that sex is a great ending to a love story.[7]

We're cheaters if we buy that. We're cheating ourselves and we're cheating our lovers – literally and figuratively, of the beautiful, delightful, joyful, precious, good love.

Screwtape again. Some advice to his nephew concerning agape and marriage:

> In other words, the humans are to be encouraged to regard as the basis for marriage a highly coloured and distorted version of something the Enemy really promises as its result. Two advantages follow … they regard the intention of loyalty to a partnership for mutual help, for the preservation of chastity, and for the transmission of life, as something lower than a storm of emotion. In the second place any sexual infatuation whatever, so long as it intends marriage, will be regarded as "love" and "love" will be held to excuse a man from all the guilt, and to protect him from all the consequences of marrying a heathen, a fool, or a wanton.[8]

Once we view eros as an indicator of agape rather than a result of agape, we head down the slippery path Screwtape (and mediocrity) want us on. We start to view a storm of sexual emotion as more important than loyalty and partnership. We start to raise the value of emotion to something close to true love.

So, we marry because we have some great naked time together. And that means nothing.

Nothing.

And we wonder why the marriage doesn't work?

Love is a storm of emotion instead of the committing, sacrificial love that agape is.

Doesn't sacrificial love just feel right?
Doesn't sacrificial love touch you deep in your bones?

love is fruit

When someone says they love you, don't you want that to mean that they care more about how you feel than how they feel?

Doesn't that seem like something that would head us toward the road to ...

Beautiful.
Delightful.
Joyful.
Precious.
Good?

It's not the most romantic thing you've ever heard, but it goes something like this: A wife asks her husband, after fifty years of marriage, "Why do you still love me?" The husband replies, "Because I promised I would."

We've been programmed to think the husband should say, "Because you are more beautiful to me than ever," or, "Because my heart still skips a beat every time you walk into the room."

We've been taught that "Because I promised I would" isn't that great.

We're taught by mediocrity.

"Because I promised I would" should make our hearts melt because it's so damn powerful.

I think back to the old story. The one about her and him and the whispering voice. I wonder if some of the good fruit was agape. Mediocrity didn't want her to eat that fruit.

So he recommended the forbidden, crappy fruit to her: the easier one. The flashier one. The one that looked like it tasted better. She bought the lie and took a bite of eros.

We're still taking big bites of the same fruit today.

Agape satisfies a relationship. The others, by themselves, don't.

If there is agape there will be eros, philia, and storge. Agape doesn't rest if they aren't there. Agape is the steak that brings the carrots, lettuce, and dressing into a nourishing meal.

Agape isn't satisfied with two out of three. It will look for and discover why the sex isn't heating up the bedroom, the friendship isn't the one that overrules all others, and the affectionate touches on the cheek and collarbone aren't there.

It will work tirelessly to bring them.

Agape makes anything else that tries to approach its level look downright tired and lame.

Agape makes everything pale in comparison, because there's nothing in the world like it.

Agape *moves* our body, our mind, and our soul. I think it *moves* all three back toward ...

Beautiful.
Delightful.
Joyful.
Precious.
Good.

John Chrysostom lived in 400 A.D. They called him "The Golden Mouth" because he was an amazing speaker.

> The beauty of the body, if it is not joined with virtue of the soul, will be able to hold a husband for twenty or thirty days, but will go no farther before it shows its wickedness and destroys all its attractiveness ... [9]

The beauty of the body joined with the virtue of the soul.

An amazing line and powerful thought.

Without the beauty of the body and the virtue of the soul together, Chrysostom says we have twenty to thirty days of alright, mediocre, sex followed by the destruction of all attractiveness ... obviously leading to damaged people and destruction. It's hard to believe he spoke the

love is fruit

words over 1,600 years ago.

A lot of relationships today consisting of twenty to thirty days of alright sex followed by the destruction of all attractiveness.

In fact, relationships that consist of twenty to thirty days of alright sex have somehow become synonymous with love for many. For some it is the best of what they expect to ever have.

Mediocrity lived out to the full.

slum
Slumdog Millionaire. I absolutely love the movie. Most of us have this top ten list of movies in our heads and, for me, Slumdog is on it. Probably top five.

It punched me in the gut, delighted my eyes, and moved me in a way that not many movies do. It's a love story, but not like most love stories.

It's not an eros story but it is an agape story.

It is a story of sacrifice, of forgiveness, and a story of a wild love that will stop for nothing.

It is a story of hardships, of trouble, and of despair … but a story of true, real, deep, love.

There is this scene: Jamal (the main character) is standing in front of Latika (the woman he loves). He reaches his hand to reveal a scar on the side of Latika's cheek. It is a scar that represents the pain of what so much of the movie is about. It's a pain that represents mistakes, represents jealousy, represents betrayal, and represents lots of surface loves. Jamal leans down and kisses the scar in a symbolic gesture of what his love means to her.

The mistakes are gone, the jealousy is over, the betrayal has vanished and the surface loves are petty.

Add in a nice soundtrack and some gorgeous cinematography and I'm crying.

It's moving to see. Agape always is.

We've become convinced that love is sex. Love is nice friends. Love is a little innocence.

I love you, what does it mean?

> I want to masturbate inside of you.
>
> or
>
> You are my best friend whom I want to caress as though there is nothing more important in the world because I promise to appreciate the virtue of your soul along with the beauty of your body and if we have sex in the process it will be something that strikes us at our deepest and most intimate levels of humanity.

I love you.

They can be such powerful words.

This chapter started out with definitions. Agape is the definition of love. As we move forward, and talk about love, agape is what we mean.

The word that mediocrity doesn't want us to consider.

The fruit that mediocrity is working hard to distract us from.

love is fruit

Agape never fails.

*Anyone can become angry – that is easy.
But to become angry with the right person,
to the right degree,
at the right time,
for the right purpose,
and in the right way – that is not easy.
That requires some thought.*

Aristotle

eight. mangos.

I love mangos. There isn't a fruit that comes close to them, in my opinion.

If a fruit can be sexy, mangoes are: sweet to the tongue, juicy, and exciting. They have that whole tropical thing going for them. Unique. Flavorful. One of a kind.

Apples? Boring.

Bananas? Americans eat more bananas per year than apples and oranges combined.[1]

Boring.

Mangos? They stand out.

Whatever your favorite fruit is, start thinking about it. Start salivating over it. Remember how good it tastes going down and how satisfied and full you feel after you've eaten it.

If fruit is love and sex and all things in between, I think we're all after a satisfying, tasty, juicy and exciting fruit. We're all after that agape stuff. Good fruit isn't easy or cheap. Living in the Pacific Northwest, mangos are rare. They are expensive. They aren't in every grocery store, but, oh man, when we get one in our house – a little bit of heaven.

This whole conversation is not about a punishment, but reward.

Apples and bananas are everywhere ... are there any mangos?[2]

If you take the Aristotle quote on the opposite page and then do a little interpretation, it goes something like this:

> Anyone can have sex. That's easy. But to have sex with the right person, to the right degree, at the right time, for the right purpose, and in the right way – that

is not easy. That requires some thought.

The *right* person, the *right* degree, the *right* time, the *right* purpose, and the *right* way.

That's a lot of *rights*.

Anyone can have sex with the *wrong* person, to the *wrong* degree, at the *wrong* time, with the wrong purpose, and in the wrong way. I once worked with a very heavy, very acne covered, very gross dishwasher who would use his entire paycheck every two weeks to pay for women to have sex with him.

Trust me, anyone can have sex.

The question becomes do you believe there is a better fruit?

Do you believe there is better sex than most people are having? Than you're having?

Do you believe there is optimus (Latin for "the best") sex?

If you don't, join the crowds. Keep repeating the lie until they believe it … There are obviously enough of us who believe the lies about the apple hanging off the tree while ignoring that delicious mango a little further away.

As Aristotle said, all those "rights" require some thought. They require us to realize that the wrongs are affecting more than us. They are killing our system of love and relationship, and throwing out boomerangs.

The rights? What are those? Maybe we can get this thing back toward mangos and optimus.

soul sex
When my wife and I were trying to have our third child, things didn't go as easy as they did with the first two. As a result, I was introduced to something called "baby sex." Baby sex, in its simplest form, is sex to have a baby. Pure and simple, unadulterated procreation.

Procreation is not that sexy of a word.

mangos

The plan was for my wife to check her "ovulation calendar" and inform me the days we needed to have sex. During those days, the plan was to procreate. On the surface, this sounded like one of the best plans ever conceived by a human being, let alone a woman, let alone my wife. I was 100% on board. Could it get any better?

An unexpected thing happened. It wasn't that amazing.

It was missing something.

Sex, missing something? Is that possible?

Yes.

We know men want sex. It's obvious. But, men don't want *just* sex. They want something else. A report released in 2007 indicated that 38% of men who cheated did so because they wanted more satisfying sex.[3]

Is it possible to have more satisfying sex? How?

I thought women were just a receptacle for semen and the same as masturbation? (Maybe this is where us humans are not like animals.)

I think men really want sex with a woman who wants to have sex. Men may act like they don't care but that's just not the case. Men want a woman who wants a man.

They want a woman who doesn't just want sex from a man, but the man himself.

They don't want a woman who has sex to get him off her back so she can enjoy the rest of her evening. They don't want a woman who has sex because she's scared what would happen if she doesn't. They don't even want a woman who is just looking for a good f---.

Yeah, they say they do. But we don't. Not deep in our soul.

We fall into the trap of thinking it's just the sex, but it's not. We start to believe that coercing our girlfriend into giving us sex is good. We start to believe that Cancun sex, on boats with drunk girls who can't make decisions is good, or that a wife who gives us sex out of duty is good. We start to believe that wild and crazy chick who we meet in the bar and slam against the bathroom stall is good.

None of them are. Thinking so, just moves us down the path of mediocrity.

I have a friend who puts it this way: "I'm most happy when my wife has a desire for me sexually."

That's very different from Cancun.

There is another thing we have to acknowledge: men are a lot more into her feelings than we let ourselves believe.

We want *her* to be happy and content and blissful. Not just sexually. Her whole body, her mind, and her spirit. We pretend we don't, and we fall for all kinds of lame alternatives that leave us unsatisfied in the end.

But, we really do.

If you're a man and you think it's just about the sex, stop for a second and really think about it. Honestly.

For all of the talk about using a woman as a receptacle for sperm, you want more and you know it. You want *way* more. The problem is that you have become so controlled by lies, by other men, and by pressure to eat all this crap mediocrity is feeding us that you don't stop to look at the bars that are being built around you: the bars of short term thrills. Stop for a second and look at the cage. It's there and it's getting higher and thicker, and soon it will be too high for you to crawl out of.

But you want out. You want agape. You want soul sex. Are you really going to keep convincing yourself that you don't?

Author and speaker Rob Bell once said, "the skin is connected to the soul."

Think about that one for a second. If the skin is connected to the soul, the things we do to our skin affects our souls. Maybe the first things that come to mind are all the negative ways. The bad, forbidden fruits.

And that's true. That's the frightening part.

But, what if the "right" and positive things we do to the skin benefit our souls in a positive way?

That could be amazing.

Can treating your skin the right way, affect your soul in a positive way? Can having sex at the right time, to the right degree, with the right purpose and with the right person actually bring some beauty, joy, delight, goodness, and something precious to the deeper, inward parts of our being?

That's amazing, if it's true.

Another great author. Frederick Buechner:

> Contrary to Mrs. Gundy, sex is not a sin. Contrary to Hugh Hefner, it's not salvation either. Like nitroglycerine it can be used either to blow up bridges or heal hearts. At its root the hunger for food is the hunger for survival. At its root the hunger to know a person sexually is the hunger to know and be known by the person humanly. Food without nourishment doesn't fill the bill for long, and neither does sex without humanness.[4]

Sex without humanness. Knowing and being known. Bones of my bone and flesh and flesh of my flesh.

The deep stuff. The real stuff. The truly satisfactory stuff.

Are we moving toward it or away from it?

seventy-two
There is a fairly popular book that talks about "the 72 hour rule."[5] The "rule" says that it's a biological need for men to ejaculate every 72 hours.

THE NAKED FRUIT

Call me crazy, but I'm not buying it.

In my opinion, men don't *have* to have sex. We *want* to have sex, but we won't die if we don't. In fact, we probably won't even get uncomfortable. I'm not saying that thinking you are going to have sex and then not having it isn't uncomfortable, nor I am going to say that it's not easy to get irritated. But, the last thing a man needs is another reason to have sex or to get pissed off that he didn't get it.

That all comes naturally enough.

Military personnel are away from their wives for a year. I don't have proof and *Jarhead* didn't give me much evidence, but I'm fairly certain there are some men who don't jack off and look at porn even while not having sex in the military for nine-month stays.

Priests and monks don't have sex for their entire lives. While quite a few sickos have ruined the name "priest" by having sex with altar boys, and anyone else they can take advantage of, there are thousands of other incredibly wise and gifted men who have not ruined the name and have managed to live for 60, 70, 80, and 90 years without having sex.

I had the chance to hear the author Shane Claiborne speak[6] and during his talk he quoted a friend of his who was a monk who had taken a vow of celibacy. The quote went something like this:

> Any man can live without sex.
>
> No man can live without love.
>
> There are a lot of people in this world having a lot of sex but they don't have any love.
>
> There are a lot of people in this world who have a lot of love and don't have any sex.

I wonder if you believe that. Remember the definitions of love?

Agape? Eros?

Can you live without love? Without agape?

mangos

Can you live without sex? Without Eros?

Which one are you going to find in a strip club
                              in pornography,
                                    in Cancun?

I wonder if any of this has to do with the reasons that 13 to 24-year-olds say that sex makes them less happy. It's not a happy feeling to discover you didn't get love, humanness, and being known, when you thought you were going to.

All of this leads to another lie: A man won't love a woman unless she has sex with him.

The logic tells her that if she wants to keep him she'd better have sex with him.

The logic tells him that if a she doesn't have sex with him, she's not interested.

I just read a couple of books, written by guys who like to tell women all the reasons they need to have sex with them. Here's one thing they had to say to women:

> A man isn't "into you" if he's not having sex with you.[7]
>
> If a man doesn't want to have sex with you ... drop him or get it somewhere else. That's what men do.[8]

Make the lie big, make it simple, keep saying it, and eventually they will believe it.

in the pudding
In the '80s, the movie *Say Anything* became famous for the scene where the main character holds up his radio to the window of the girl he wants to date and plays "In Your Eyes." Awesome song and a great scene.

More important, though, is the fact that men will, indeed, say anything.

Pearl Jam fan. Well, I'm into Keith Urban now.

Love McDonalds? Actually, The Vegan House.

Monday Night Football tonight? Can't, going to watch Grey's Anatomy.

It was always confusing until a girl came into the picture who was a country music fan, a vegan, or a Grey's lover. Then it would all make sense. After the relationship ended, the Keith Urban CD, tofu recipes, and poster of Derek and Meredith were in the trash.

Say anything. Act any way.

If he thinks she will react to it, he will say it, eat it, or act it. Part of that is cool. At least it shows some effort.

But, there is a problem. If he'll say anything and do anything to make her think what he thinks she wants him to think, how does anyone know if he's telling the truth? In other words, how does anyone prove they are truly after the long term and not just pretending to in order to get the cheap thrill?

And if we can never prove any of this are we ever going to get back to what we're trying to get back to?

> The proof is in the pudding.

> Talk is cheap.

> Actions speak louder than words.

Prove it.

Though we will act, eat, or say just about anything, we won't *do* just about anything. And there's one thing in particular that a man won't do if he's after a cheap thrill. There's one thing a man won't do if he's using a woman as a means to end and pretending not to.

A good way to determine what kind of fruit we are after, as men, is to not have sex until we know there is agape.

mangos

There are easy questions to answer. If you're a man, ask yourself:

> What if I were just getting a kiss here and there in my relationship?
>
> Would I leave?
>
> Or, is there something more that I'm after here, like her?
>
> Would she leave?

If you're a woman ask yourself:

> What if I were just giving him a kiss here and there in our relationship?
>
> Would he leave?
>
> Or, is there something more that he's after here, like me?
>
> Would I leave?

There are lots of men who have dumped girls for being "prudes." I'll admit that I have. I would hope those girls are now happy I did. They were better off without me. There will be many men who continue to dump girls for being "prudes."

When my wife and I were dating, we went through what could be called a "prude" time. Funny, I never thought once about ending our relationship. It was the furthest thing from my mind, because agape was growing and I knew it. She was worth it. There was something deeper at work. She knew it and I knew it, and there was nothing that would stop the pursuit of that something.

It was too beautiful.

let it sleep
There was once a King named Solomon. Very wealthy, very smart, and a very good writer. He wrote a great love story and in the story he

THE NAKED FRUIT

talked a lot about fruit. He said stuff like this:

> Like an apple tree among the trees of the forest
> is my lover among the young men.
>
> Your plants are an orchard of pomegranates
> with choice fruits.[9]
>
> Let my lover come into his garden
> and taste its choice fruits.[10]
>
> Your stature is like that of the palm,
> and your breasts like clusters of fruit.[11]

If it's not clear, the fruit in Solomon's story is not really about apples, pomegranates, and grapes. You could say that Solomon's culture was similar to the culture that wrote the story of Adam and Eve.

It's not really about apples.

There is a line in Solomon's story that female character repeats quite a bit.

> But my own vineyard is mine to give.[12]

Translated: My body and my fruit (and we all know what fruit we're talking about here) are mine. I'll give it to who I want, when I want and where I want. And if you want it, you'll have to prove, that you deserve it.

In his story, there's another line that Solomon repeats over and over. As the couple is beginning the early stages of love, Solomon says this line quite a few times:

> Do not arouse or awaken love until it so desires.[13]

The word Solomon used for love in his language is the equivalent of eros.

In other words, what Solomon was saying was:

120

> Do not arouse or awaken sexuality/sexual love until it
> so desires.

Is that strange to you? He didn't say awaken eros when *he* desires or when *she* desires or when your friends desire. He said awaken sexual love when *it* desires.

How can sexual love desire anything?
Sex doesn't have the ability to desire, does it?

burn
Have you ever seen a forest fire?

While our family was camping a few years ago we watched (with binoculars) a fire grow from its infancy, a small trail of smoke, into a roaring wall of fire that ate up the mountain opposite the lake where we were staying. The night sky glowed orange and the day sky was shaded with smoke.

Fire like that is one of the most powerful things you'll see: all-consuming.

The potential of sex is powerful in a similar way. It can be an all-consuming energy. It can be passionate. It can be explosive. Eros can explode in the same way a massive forest fire does. When the situation is right, eros awakens. Eros does desire.

But we probably knew this already. We know sex carries an energy. We know sex is powerful.

Why did Solomon warn us to not unleash the power until it is ready? Why would anyone say not to enjoy the power of sex with the drunk girls in Cancun? If it's fun, it's fun. And no one is going to say that having sex with drunk girls in Cancun isn't fun right?

Is it possible that there is something with more power out there?
Is it possible that unleashing the power early, and in the wrong places and wrong times, reduces the power?

Is it possible that when we start a fire and then extinguish it, something happens?

Something that moves it toward mediocrity and away from optimal?

Maybe starting a fire for a weekend in Cancun and extinguishing it when everyone gets back to school, takes energy. Maybe if we light a fire for a few days in a hotel room and then snuff it out with a goodbye peck on the cheek, it won't burn as bright the next time?

As the exotic dancer said, maybe a wall is put up.

Science says that whenever two people engage in close and intimate contact, or sexual activity, the neurochemical oxytocin is released in the female brain, causing the woman to feel a bond to the man, whether he is a jerk or not. In the same way, the neurochemical vasopressin does the same thing to a man: makes him feel a bond to the woman whether she is a great match or not.[14]

The two chemicals released at the wrong time can have an affect.

> ... they cannot know they are seriously damaging a bonding mechanism that they are born with, a mechanism put there to allow them to, in the future, have a healthy bonded marriage that is a stable relationship ... [15]

In other words lighting that fire and extinguishing it, damages us. It damages our future potential of relationships and sex.

Rob Bell wrote a great book called *Sex God*. In it, he says this:

> What goes on between them is a profound mystery. The mystery of the mingling of souls ... When it is shared with others, it no longer belongs to them exclusively. And its power is decreased. Because the power of their coming together is rooted in their choice to give themselves to each other and to no one else in this particular way.
>
> Its power is derived from its exclusivity.
>
> That's why wedding ceremonies stir us like they do. The bride comes down the aisle and gives herself to

this man and no one else. They have something with each other that they have with no one else.

We have to be careful what we share. Because when you give it away, you no longer have it.[16]

Its power is derived from its exclusivity.

Think about the opposite of that statement.

On average men have sex with thirteen partners and women with seven.[17]

Is that power? Is that awakening sex when it desires? Does that lead to optimal or mediocre?

There is a popular statement:

> Sex is not the search for something that's missing. It's the expression of something that's been found.

I wonder if we will ever be truly satisfied with so much searching.

exclusivity +
Exclusivity is another one of those words. Its definition is confusing in our culture.

We want the exclusive invitation to the club, the exclusive deal on the vacation package, or the exclusive interview.

Why don't we want exclusive sex? Or do we?

(On a side note, you can play a similar definition game with the word innocent.)

Some say that the ancient Jewish culture believed in exclusivity with such intensity that they viewed sex and marriage as the same thing. When you had sex with someone, you married them. You became one. In other words, you had sex and you were suddenly pledged to take care of one another for life. You were joined in every way. Why?

Because they knew that you had already joined souls and souls don't break apart very easily. They recognized the connection between the skin and soul, and they knew that once souls had been joined together everyone in the culture would be happier if those souls were exclusively tied together for life.

What would happen if you viewed sex as equal to marriage?

> Would you marry the girl in the bar after knowing her for one night?
>
> Would you marry the drunk chick on spring break who was lifting her shirt for your friend?
>
> Would you marry the girl you never really thought was that cute but she was easy?
> Would you marry the guy who bought you the nice tequila?
>
> Would you marry the next guy who comes through the hotel door who can offer you a bit of attention for a few days?

For thousands of years, marriage has been the litmus test for agape.

Marriage, though it has become quite a bit less today, was always meant to be a ceremony indicating agape. That's why it happened. And, to this day, I have not seen better evidence for agape than marriage, especially a marriage where the couple getting married has not had sex.

If you have seen better evidence for agape, I'm happy to listen. Honestly.

Gisele Bündchen, New England Patriots quarterback Tom Brady's girlfriend, said, "Today, no one is a virgin when they get married."

Since another woman was pregnant with Tom Brady's child when she said it, maybe it made Gisele feel better.

But it's the same old thing: rip the virgin or act like they are the weird ones. It reminds me of my high school days. The days where everyone calls out the virgins as the weird ones even though there are more virgins at graduation than people who are not.[18]

But it's fun to call the virgins names.

Nerd.
Gay.
Prude.
Never got a chance.
Loser.
Geek.
Religious nut.
Missing out.

I wonder if there are other types of people who choose virginity.

People who don't like cages.
People who don't like cheap facsimiles.
People who don't like mediocrity.
People who like the power of exclusivity.
People who think the people who call them all of the above names are just jealous.

Of course, these people want to have sex, but that's not really the point. As Aristotle insinuated, anyone can have sex if they want to.

Big deal.

Virgins might want something better.

There are men who believe that there are better ways to show a woman you are "into them" than screwing them and dumping them a few weeks later.

There are women who actually believe that their vineyard is their own and they will give it when they want to. And if you think differently, they'll have to, as Avril Lavigne once sang, kick your ass.

There are people who don't think "missing out" is actually missing out.

rebel angels

I have a son who is a football fanatic. He's a Seattle Seahawks fan and he grew up watching their MVP running back Shaun Alexander.

My son was reading Shaun Alexander's book a couple of years ago, and he came downstairs to tell us what he had just read. He read that Shaun Alexander didn't even kiss his wife until the day they were married. [19]

Kiss?

Kiss.

Are you sure?

The story goes that Shaun's wife-to-be came to him and said she didn't think they should kiss until they were married.

Think about our normal responses to such a proposal. Of course not. Why would I do that? We need to connect physically before we're married. Guys *need* to kiss. (And much more.)

I'm not …

A Nerd.
Gay.
A Prude.
A Loser.
A Geek.
A Religious nut.
Missing out.

It's interesting where our thoughts immediately go and what that tells us about how much influence mediocrity has on our system.

Very rarely do we hear that and say

Do you value her?
Do you respect her?
Would you do anything for her?

mangos

Shaun agreed to her proposal. The first kiss they ever gave each other was after they heard the words, "You may kiss your bride." Shaun writes in his book, "It was worth it."

It was?

Is that even possible?

Really?

Kevin Roose was a college student at Brown University. He decided to go undercover and live at Liberty University, one of the most conservative universities in the country, for a semester to see what it was like. He wrote a great book about his experiences. He found a university with rules on dating, rules on drinking and rules on everything else.

It's interesting that toward the end of the book he writes this about the Liberty rules on dating, rules which included a prohibition on kissing:

> At first I thought "The Liberty Way" and its rules against physical contact would ruin the dating experience. But strangely, I'm not feeling frustrated on these dates. In fact, having preordained physical boundaries takes a huge amount of pressure and anxiety out of the process ... And that's a very freeing feeling. When dinner dates aren't just preludes to hooking up, you end up truly listening to each other. The conversation is the centerpiece, and what emerges is deeper and more intimate than if you had been spending your time trying to Don Juan your way into her bed.[20]

It was freeing?

I have a friend who played football at the University of Washington when they won the National Championship. He told a story about a girlfriend, whom he had not been dating long, suddenly laying on his bed naked when he came out of the bathroom one evening. He turned around and said, "I don't know what I did to make you think I wanted that, but you should put your clothes on."

She should?

I know a guy who drove his date home from the homecoming dance and dropped her off. It was the first date they had gone on, but the girl was begging him to come in and go to her bedroom. He walked her to the door and said no thanks.

No thanks?

I know another guy who was at a bachelor party a few years ago. All the guys were going to a strip club, so he called his wife and had her pick him up.

Pick you up?

Let me make myself clear: I'm not saying that we should stop kissing or stop dating. There are plenty of other books for that and I'm not writing any of them. In fact, I'm pretty convinced that all those things do is distract us from the bigger problem.

But why is our first reaction always to laugh and call it ridiculous. How do you know? Have you ever tried it?

Why are *they* the prudes, nerds, idiots, and losers and *we* are the free, cool, smart, winners?

I was out for lunch with a college junior and he told me how bad he wants a girlfriend who will "own him."

Own you?

We talked some more and he said that he wanted a girl who was in control. Tough. Not easy. A girl who would make him earn it. He said, "I want a rebel" but "a rebel who is an angel." He wants a girl who isn't going along with whatever he wants and whatever society wants.

We talked some more, and I said, "If women only knew how bad the decent guys want the girl that acts as though she has no need for him." To which he nodded and responded, "You always want what you can't have."

I wonder if that's why we make fun of people who have something we don't.

mangos

We don't need another "Just Say No" campaign, that's for sure.

Maybe we need a "Just Say Yes" campaign.

It's about what good is out there to get.
It's about getting back to Eden.
It's about getting back to …
Beautiful.

Delightful.

Joyful.

Precious and Good.

It was worth it.

It was freeing.

Put your clothes on.

No thanks.

Honey, can you pick me up?

I want a rebel angel.

Mangos.

*A day may come when the courage of men fails,
when we forsake our friends
and break all bonds of fellowship,
but it is not this day.
An hour of woes and shattered shields,
when the age of men comes crashing down!
But it is not this day!
This day we fight!
By all that you hold dear on this good Earth,
I bid you stand, Men of the West!*

Aragorn, The Lord of the Rings

nine. hero.

Aragorn.

Neo.

Leonidas.

Superman.

Heroes.

The definition:

> A person, typically a man, who is admired or idealized for courage, outstanding achievements, or noble qualities.

It's easy to love the person who fights through the problems and negatives in his or her life (which usually accost a hero) and ends up, by doing right, conquering the powerful villains who are trying to destroy him or her, and, in the end, saving the world.

Who doesn't love the person who sacrifices themselves for the good of everyone else? Who doesn't love brave King Leonidas when he fights to the death against a much larger, better equipped army, standing firm in his beliefs until the end? Who doesn't love Captain Kirk, willing to lay down his life for the lives of his crew? Who doesn't love Aragorn giving his speech to the horsemen and charging down the hill into the midst of the armies of Sauron when there is little hope they can win?

Why are hero movies often the top money makers?
Why is any story (fiction or non) about a hero almost irresistible?

We said earlier that men like to fight for something, and that's part of it. We want a cause, a mission, a purpose. But it's more than that.

Many people have causes.

Many people like the *idea* of fighting, of sacrificing, of nobility. A lot of Scotsmen thought that freedom for Scotland was a great idea. Unfortunately, they stayed at home in their beds, thinking about the idea and how much they liked it. William Wallace made his beliefs real by putting them into action.

William Wallace was a hero not because he *wanted* something but because he *did* something.

Heroes don't just want something. They do something.
They don't just believe in something. They act on that belief.

Many people want true love. Many people want soul sex. Many people would rather claim optimus than mediocrity. Many people would rather have the best in life than a second-rate imitation.

It's easy to want good things. It's not always easy to get them. In fact, it's hard to fight for the things we believe in. It's a pain.

A friend of mine once said:

> The pain of doing the right thing will never be as strong as the pain of regret.[1]

Another one of those rights.

It's a pain to do the right thing. We have no problem admitting that one.

It's a pain not to do the right thing. We don't like to admit that one because mediocrity doesn't want us to.

Twilight again. In the stories, Edward is the vampire. Yeah, he drinks blood and jumps through the air and lives forever, but I was more intrigued with another aspect to him: Edward can't be too close to the woman he loves. He can't kiss her too long. He must be in control at all times when around her. If he loses that control, he knows he will not be able to contain himself and he will hurt her. He knows he could kill her.

The illustration is powerful: Edward is a man, like most men, who wants

hero

to have his way with the woman of his dreams. He resists and controls himself because he knows, while fulfilling his short-term desires, in the end, it would harm the one person in the world he doesn't want to harm.

Edward fights against his short-term desires because he is fighting for his ultimate desire.

It's interesting how much more likely we, as a society, are to accept the story as long as Edward is a vampire. But if Edward were a normal person with normal desires that will harm his normal girlfriend, suddenly we, as a society, call Edward all kinds of names and laugh at his fight for true love, his willingness to not take what he wants because it will hurt someone.

We don't believe a normal man can bring as much harm as a vampire.

Keep repeating the lie. Eventually we'll believe it.

But we have to believe it's the right thing and we have to believe there will be regret.

We have to be willing to fight for the right thing and to fight to avoid the regret.

Not too long ago I was with a man who said, "You always hear that time heals all wounds. I don't know. It was how many years ago now, but the more time that goes by and the more I think about what I did, the more regret I have. I wish I had fought harder."

Heroes are willing to fight. For themselves and for others.

Heroes are willing to fight for beauty.
Heroes are willing to fight for delightful.
Heroes are willing to fight for joyful.
Heroes are willing to fight for precious.
Heroes are willing to fight for good.

Are you?

THE NAKED FRUIT

dumb and dumber
Morality.
Rules.
Laws.
Guidelines.

As we said already, we generally don't like those words, or any words associated with them. I'm not sure why we don't like them because no matter whether we like them or not, we all live by them.

I've never met a person yet who doesn't.

We may not agree on what is wrong and right but we all think it's one or the other. This person thinks it's wrong to have sex with three girls at once. This one doesn't. This one thinks it's wrong to look at porn. This one doesn't.

It's not just the person who thinks it's wrong that has morality. It's anyone who is making a judgment on anything as to whether it is wrong or right.

But, like most things mediocrity gets his fangs into, he manipulates and twists and turns morality into something that puts a bad taste in our mouth. We start to look at words like morality and rules and start to believe the sole reason they exist is to take away all fun and joy from our planet. We start to believe they are conservative, religious, parental, or just plain boring even though we all live by them already.

We all live with morality because we've known morality all along.

Jonah Lehrer, a Rhodes scholar who worked with Nobel-prize-winning neuroscientist Eric Kandel, says,

> The details of the Ten Commandments reflect the details of the evolved moral brain.[2]

It's not as though religion came along and invented some rules and our brain followed along. Lehrer says our brains and emotions were already there and it is religion that followed along and put them into writing.

Mediocrity doesn't like morality, so he makes it complicated and confusing. It's probably not though.

Jonah Lehrer again:

> Moral decisions require taking other people into account ... Doing the right thing means thinking about everybody else, using the emotional brain to mirror the emotions of strangers.[3]

In other words morality, at its base, is taking a moment to think of how others feel. It's taking a moment to think about how we would feel and placing those feelings on to the person we are affecting.

Morality is asking how *you* feel instead of how *I* feel.

We all do this. All the time. In order to determine right and wrong, we all, to some degree or another, must, at some point, think about someone else.

The only question is how we think about them.

the big one
Don't have sex before you are married.

We have lots of labels for the statement and those who say it.

Stupid.
Conservative.
Out-of-touch.
Old fashioned.
Boring.
(Fill in the blank.)

And many of us believe we will prove the stupid, conservative, out-of-touch, boring, (fill in the blank) person wrong with the way we live.

If the rule was created by someone or something, we could be on to something. If, however, the rule comes from a deeper spot, from something we've always known to be true or to feel right, something our brains created in the first place, we could be in trouble.

THE NAKED FRUIT

It's hard to prove wrong what we've always know to be right.

We take other rules like "don't look at porn" and "don't have an affair" and "don't go to strip clubs" and do the same.

But if we go back to the idea that the rules were first written out because they detailed something that was already going on in who we are as humans, we start to see things differently. Maybe the rules are there for a different reason from the reason our buddy the swinging bachelor bartender tells us.

Maybe the "rules" came about because deep inside we know something true about them: they bring damage to us and to others. If you look at what most of the "rules" prohibit, you find that almost every one of them damages relationships between human beings in some form or another. The more we damage relationships, the more we damage the system we're all living in.

Maybe these rules were never about making our lives boring, but making them better. Better relationships make better marriages, bringing better sex and better love and better lives.

We've tried a long time to prove these things wrong. Are we winning?

According to the author Mary Eberstadt, who happens to be an atheist, no:

> If our Movement is really going to go around arguing that the sooner we get rid of all those rules, the happier humanity is going to be, we're going to get blown away by this kind of counterevidence ... [4]

Have you ever heard a happily married man or woman (the kind who have the type of marriage that we all really want) say something like,

> Boy I wish I had a lot more sex in high school. That was really stupid of me. What was I thinking? If only I could go back. My spouse is great but what was I thinking?

On the other hand, have you ever heard happily married men and women, and many unmarried, say,

> Boy, I wish I hadn't had sex with that girl or guy. If there is one thing I could change in my life it would be that.

I have.

I have heard lots of people say that one and it often ends up being followed by something like, "If there is one thing I'm going to make sure my kids know … "

So those rules and guidelines keep going because we all realize that some things are deeper than our short-term thrills.

I would argue that we all realize it, whether we're taught it or not. I would argue that another one of the reasons teens would say that sex makes them less happy in the long term is because it's breaking something deep inside of them that is not supposed to be broken.

Of course, not everyone agrees.

odds
I guess there's a chance that someone could have great sex with the entire cheerleading squad and bring back beauty. I suppose there's a chance that we could cheat on our wife or husband and bring back delight. Maybe there is a chance that we could live at the strip club and bring back precious. It's possible we could look at porn everyday before tucking our three daughters into bed and bring back joy.

In fact, there are numerous authors who write books about the hundreds of women they have sex with, the hundreds of positions they try, the hundreds of places they do it, and how damn happy they are in the process.

That's great.

Will any one of the cheerleaders regret having sex with them? Will our husband or wife appreciate us cheating on them? Will the stripper be affected by us watching her night after night? Will the girl making the porn we are looking at be affected? Will our three daughters appreciate us looking at porn?

In other words, the numerous authors who write the books … supposing there is no regret for them, I wonder how often do they go back and talk to the hundreds of women they've had sex with to see if there is any regret there?

Moral decisions require taking other people into account. Do we? Are you?

Or are we breaking down the system even more?

Jim Carrey played Lloyd in the movie *Dumb and Dumber.* Lloyd was in love with a girl that was not in love with him and at one point Llloyd asks the girl he was in love with if she would ever marry him.

> "No."
>
> Lloyd replies, "What are the odds?"
>
> "A million to one."
>
> Lloyd responds in his classic Jim Carrey slow, dumb voice, "So ... you're saying there is a chance ... "

Maybe, just maybe, you'll be the one to prove morality wrong. I've never met anyone who has but maybe you could be the one in a million who does. I personally don't like playing the odds. But even if I did, there's another aspect.

The value at the end.

No one cares if you've got great odds to win five bucks. If you've got good odds to win a thousand I'll start to pay attention. If we're talking about love, there is no monetary comparison.

What Happens in Vegas was a movie that brought out some interesting questions, and my favorite one was this: Would you not have sex with your girlfriend until you were married if someone promised you 3 million dollars on your wedding day?

If 3 million is the payout, people start giving it consideration. For 3 million, people might wait. What about for 1 million?

hero

The question quickly becomes, How much is your wife worth? Your husband? Your marriage? Your virginity? Beautiful? Delight? Good?

Given the statistics, it seems that most people don't view their spouse or marriage as worth anything close to a million dollars.

What is beautiful, good, joyful, precious, or delightful about that?

Bono, of U2 fame, said this:

> Rebellion starts at home, in your heart, in your refusal to compromise your beliefs and your values.[5]

Rebel angels. Refusing to compromise some things.

In *The Screwtape Letters*, the demons are all gathered together, having a feast down in Hell, and Screwtape stands up to give a toast, saying:

> Then there was the lukewarm Casserole of Adulterers. Could you find it in any trace of a fully inflamed, defiant, rebellious, insatiable lust? I couldn't. They all tasted to me like undersexed morons who had blundered or trickled into the wrong beds in automatic response to sexy advertisements, or to make themselves feel modern and emancipated, or to reassure themselves about their virility or their "normalcy," or even because they had nothing else to do.[6]

Do you want to be described as an undersexed moron, blundering into bed in automatic response to sexy advertisements?

Edward could have given in to everything his body was telling him to give in to.

Neo could have taken the blue pill.

King Leonidas could have bowed to the king of Persia.

What do you want people to say about you?

What are you going to do about it?

This is where we hold them.
This is where we fight.
This is where they die.

King Leonidas, 300

ten. this is where.

Seth Godin calls it the lizard brain.[1] I like that.

Lizards are a lot like snakes. Since this whole story is about me and you and a snake that is whispering lies, the lizard brain seems to work perfectly.

What is the lizard brain? It's the part of your brain that worries about survival and anger and sex and fear. It's the older part of the brain compared to the Cerebellum and Cerebrum, which are more recent. The more recent parts control reasoning, planning, recognition, movement, hearing, memory, and speech and a whole host of stuff that we think of when we think about "thinking".

I'd say the lizard brain is where mediocrity likes to talk to us.

In some ways we have one part of the brain that controls the base parts of the humanity and one part of the brain that controls the finer parts of humanity.

In some ways we have one part of our brain that focuses on short term thrills and another that controls long term consequences.

Others use the terms Elephants and Riders.[2] The Rider directs the Elephant part of the brain. The Rider is willing to make short-term sacrifices for long-term payoffs and the Elephant prefers immediate gratification.

Remember that flaw in the brain? Here's the dangerous thing: The older parts of our brain can overpower the newer parts.

When you're half naked, you're not really reasoning.

When she's touching you, you're not really planning.

When he gives you flowers and a ring, you're not really recognizing.

... when it [the lizard brain] is aroused, the other part of our brain stands little chance, particularly if we haven't trained it for these events.[3]

There was an amazing experiment run by Dan Ariely and George Loewenstein from MIT: 35 male college students were asked a series of questions pertaining to sex.[4]

Things like:

> Could you imagine having sex with a 12-year-old girl?
>
> Would you tell a woman that you loved her to increase the chance that she would have sex with you?
>
> Would you slip a woman a drug to increase the chance that she would have sex with you?
>
> Would you keep trying to have sex after your date says, "no"?
>
> Would you use a condom even if you were afraid that a woman might change her mind while you went to get it?

They answered the questions in two different states. The first answers were given in a "normal state", presumably unaroused. With the second set of answers they were asked to stimulate themselves and shown pornography while answering the same questions.

The answers changed dramatically.

> 46% of the men could now imagine being attracted to a 12-year-old girl. Up 23%.
>
> 51% of men would now tell a woman they loved her to have sex. Up 21%.
>
> 26% of men would now slip a woman a drug. Up 21%.

> 45% of men would now keep trying to have sex once his date said no. Up 25%.
>
> 60% would now still use a condom even if it meant she might change her mind. Down 26%.

Ariely and Loewenstein concluded the study with this:

> Efforts at self-control that involve raw willpower are likely to be ineffective in the face of the dramatic cognitive and motivational changes caused by arousal.

My translation?

If we're going to move back toward beauty, delight, joy, precious, and good, we're going to have to start with the realization that the time we fight is not "when [we're] half naked and deranged with desire."[5]

It's already over by then.

Leonardo DaVinci said,

> It is easier to resist at the beginning than at the end.

So, it's now. Maybe now is the time we fight. Maybe this exact moment, as you're reading this page, is the time to fight.

true
Hitler said to repeat the lies. He knew what he was talking about.

Lies are like those annoying people you meet who immediately start telling you how much money they make or how much their house cost, or how awesome they are because they did this or that. The more someone tells me how much money they have, the more I wonder if they really have any money.

Lies like to talk a lot because they know that humans naturally repel them. At first.

Truth is like another kind of person. They have this calm and intriguing coolness to them. They don't say much, and when they do, you tend to listen. They don't seem to *need* you, and because of that you are more interested. They don't tell you that they own a multibillion-dollar company or play in the NFL unless you ask. They don't care if you know because they don't need you to care. The truth is they make more money than you and they know it, even if you don't.

Lies are desperate.
Truth is confident.

Lies berate us and break down our defenses.
Truth walks away if you reject it.

Lies need you to believe in order for them to have power.
Truth smiles.

Lies pretend.
Truth knows.

Lies are nervous.
Truth waits.

Look around. Look for lies. You start to see them everywhere. Songs, movies, television, advertisements, billboards, and just about every other form of media. Begging, pleading, shouting, yelling out "look at me, look at me."

See how much fun I am having? See how great things are? Look. Over here. I'm having the best sex of all time. Every time. Really. All night long. It doesn't matter where: on beaches, in jeeps, on dance floors, in bathrooms … sometimes with people I know and sometimes with people I don't know. None of that really matters because it's always amazing. I live life with no regrets. I just go for it. And it's always worth it. The best ever. Look at how much fun I'm having. All the time. Really.

Meanwhile the truth stares at you, quiet, with that serene sense of power.

Yeah, I'm here. You'll get it someday.

This is where we hold the lies. This is where we start to kill them. Right here.

this is where

spices
Variety is the spice of life.

Is it?

It carries elements of truth. What good lie doesn't? I have three pair of Converse All-Stars because sometimes I like black, sometimes gray, and sometimes green.

But when dating books say men need variety, they generally aren't referring to Converse.

> If a man is married to a brunette with big boobs, he sometimes needs to go see a blond with small boobs.[6]

It's just a way to spice things up. It's natural. It's good.

Remember the power of exclusivity? Where does that fit in with variety?

Frederick Buechner wrote,

> Lust is the craving for salt of a man who is dying of thirst.[7]

Salt causes thirst. If you're dying of thirst, you don't want anything to make you more thirsty. So, lust, according to Buechner, is craving the worst thing that we could crave when we need its opposite.

I don't know what you think of when you hear the word lust but it's probably something visual. The English definition of lust is

> sexual desire, sexual appetite, and sexual longing.

Like the word "love", something happened when English got a hold of "lust". English focused on one aspect of lust: sex. It's an important aspect but still just one.

Lust, in its original Latin form, is pretty simple:
> a strong desire for something.

THE NAKED FRUIT

The original word referred to a strong desire for anything, including things that are good: A strong desire for friendship or a strong desire for justice.

I lust for power.

There are other good things to lust.

> my wife.
> sex with my wife.
> friendship with my wife.

There are also not-good things to lust for.

> his wife.
> sex with his wife.
> friendship with his wife.

Given the two scenarios, we start to establish that some things aren't good to lust: things that I have no right to.

> Girlfriends.
> Porn stars.
> Strippers.
> My wife's friends.
> My friend's car.
> My friend's car's garage (and attached house).

You get the picture.

Lust is a very good liar. Lust never tells the truth. Lust always says there is something better when there isn't.

Remember the fruit? Why did Eve take a bite? Those questions started coming:

> Are you really not supposed to eat that?
> Are all those other fruits you have good enough?
> Have you looked at *this* fruit?

The story says that Eve "saw it was good for eating and pleasing to the

this is where

eye." She didn't have answers for the questions.

She had a strong desire for it.

> I have something.
> I see something else.
> I compare the two.
> I desire the something else.
> The value for the thing I do have dies a little.

One example:

> I have a Honda minivan.
> I see a Toyota Land Cruiser.
> I compare my van to the SUV.
> I desire the SUV.
> I hate my van.

A different example:

> I have a wife.
> I see another woman in a magazine.
> I compare my wife's body to her body.
> I desire her body.
> The value I have for my wife dies a little.

Lust breeds discontent. It can't survive any other way. If I'm not discontent, in any way, with what I have, then why would I desire anything else?

Discontent is bad for relationships.

Saying we need variety is like saying we need lust. We need to want something else even though we have something.

Does that make any sense?

Of course, it does, we argue. The strip club doesn't make me not want my wife. In fact, it makes me think she is more sexy. The porn makes me want her more. It's not damaging. It's beneficial.

But it's a naked body. We are enjoying looking at and desiring some aspect of that body. If we weren't, why the hell would we be there? We're looking at the body – the way it dances, the way it smiles, the way it looks, the legs, the face, the breasts, the butt, the anything – and comparing to the body or bodies we know.

It's not as though our world collapses on the first night. If it did, we wouldn't go. Mediocrity knows that. Slow, stealthy, and deadly: that's the way mediocrity rolls.

Porn, strip clubs, and the girl in the thong at the beach. Look. Compare. Desire. Lose a little of the value of what we do have. There is no getting around it.

Think about it for a while and see if the truth isn't there, quiet, smiling, and asking you to test it.

As one person, addicted to pornography (the desire of a variety of women) put it

> ... so I would retreat to this little world where women were not women ... they were there to satisfy me.[8]

Where a wife is not a wife, where a girlfriend is not a girlfriend, where all of them become nothing more than an object to satisfy. Slowly, they become something no longer even human. And once something is no longer human, we don't mind throwing it away.

Ask John Mayer or Tom Leykis.

Lust doesn't forget either. The images of porn from fifteen years ago come back and cause comparisons. The dates with those girls from high school and college come back and cause comparisons. And those comparisons can cause discontentment so easily.

If you don't believe me, talk to guys who put up pictures of porn on their headboard because they need it in order to make love to their wives. Ask the men who find their wives unsatisfactory because they don't do what they've seen or experienced other women do.

It's not pretty.

this is where

No one wants to go through life hating or not appreciating the things that they have. It's miserable to think our car or house sucks. It's miserable to see the neighbor's new car and hate our own or visit the co-worker in his new home and come home to hate your own.
It's downright tragic to think your wife or husband isn't the best.
The brilliant author G.K. Chesterton.

> To complain that I could only be married once was like complaining that I had only been born once. It was incommensurate with the terrible excitement of which one was talking. It showed not an exaggerated sensibility to sex but a curious insensibility to it.[9]

three more

I brought up Dr. Cialdini's book earlier, *The Psychology of Persuasion*. Dr. Cialdini discusses something called the contrast principle:

> Simply put, if the second item is fairly different from the first, we will tend to see it as more different than it actually is.[10]

Dr. Cialdini cites an experiment with college students. Male students were shown an image of an attractive woman and asked to rate her beauty. The beauty rating came in pretty high. The same students were then shown an image of an attractive swimsuit model before being shown the image of the other woman. Students were asked to rate the attractive woman that had been shown before, after seeing the swimsuit model. Suddenly the original woman's ratings were much lower.

The same woman had grown less attractive, only because another woman had been shown. Dr. Cialdini concludes,

> We may be less satisfied with the physical attractiveness of our own lovers because of the way the popular media bombard us with examples of unrealistically attractive models.[11]

In spite of the genius recommendations in some books to shop for what we like and don't like in pornos,[12] science would seem to say that's not a good idea.

Solomon wrote that the lips of women "drip like honey" and slice "like a double-edged sword."¹³ There is no fighting the idea that we all want what isn't ours. If you're a guy you've probably already started to imagine what you want to do with lips dripping like honey. They are sweet, succulent and attractive. She is hot, sexy, and wanting you.

But Solomon also said that once you start on those lips they cut like a sword. They'll tear you up. They'll slice and dice you: your body, your heart, your mind, and your soul. That's what lust does. It stabs. It damages.

It's little, of course. But little, every time, eventually hurts.

Solomon also said of lust, it "is a highway to the grave leading down to the chambers of death."¹⁴

I haven't read that one in any dating books.

But is it true if you think about it?

Remember truth is never the noisy one.

With over 700 wives Solomon knew it well. He lived it. He understood. Do we believe him?

Do we believe the damaged hearts, the damaged emotions, the damaged minds, the damaged bodies, the dead relationships, and the dead marriages we see all around us result from the slices of lust?

The slices of lust.

One more. John Chrysostom, the golden mouth, again. When he gave the following speech, "the theater" was the equivalent to the modern-day strip club or porn shop. It was where the women took off their clothes and where the men enjoyed the show from their seats.

> If you see a shameless woman in the theater, who treads the stage with uncovered head and bold attitudes, dressed in garments adorned with gold, flaunting her soft sensuality, singing immoral songs, throwing her limbs about in the dance, and making shameless

speeches ... do you still dare to say that nothing human happens to you then? Long after the theater is closed and everyone is gone away, those images still flat before your soul, their words, their conduct, their glances, their walk, their positions, their excitation, their unchaste limbs – and as for you, you go home covered with a thousand wounds! But not alone – the whore goes with you – although not openly and visibly ... but in your heart, and in your conscience, and there within you she kindles the Babylonian furnace ... in which the peace of your home, the purity of your heart, the happiness of your marriage will be burnt up![15]

Buechner. Chesterton. Dr. Cialdini. Solomon. Chrysostom. And many others ...

The lies on variety are everywhere. It's hard not to hear them.

The truth is there too, if you listen for its whispers.

environmental policies
In the summer of 1971, Stanford University ran a famous experiment.[16] They created a fake prison in the basement of the psychology building and interviewed student volunteers who wanted to be a part of their experiment. After making sure they were stable and "normal" volunteers, coins were flipped to see who would play the guards and who would play the prisoners.

The "guards" were given uniforms and the "prisoners" were taken to a local police station where they were arrested and then escorted to the fake prison in the basement of the school. They were strip-searched and given uniforms to wear and prison ID's for their names.

Here's the weird part: On the first night the guards were waking up the prisoners at 2 a.m., making them do push-ups and putting their feet on their backs to make them more difficult. By the second morning, the prisoners were planning a revolt and lined up all their beds to block their cells. The guards who came in that morning used fire extinguishers to spray the prisoners and push them back, and then stripped prisoners naked and put the leader into solitary confinement.

THE NAKED FRUIT

As they days went on, things got worse. Prisoners who were interviewed responded with their number and not their name. Guards became more and more brutal, abusing prisoners when they thought no one was watching. In the end, the experiment had to be cut short at six days even though it had been planned to go much longer.

What's the point?

It took two days for healthy, middle-class college students to turn into arrogant, torturing prison guards or rebelling, angry, half-insane prisoners. They transformed because their environment changed: the context, the scenery, the action around them. It was a fake prison, but suddenly everyone's character changed based on what was around them.

> When it comes to interpreting other people's behavior, human beings invariably make the mistake of overestimating the importance of fundamental character traits and underestimating the importance of the situation and context.[17]

There are many sayings about friends, along the lines of:

> You are who you hang out with.

> Bad company corrupts good character.

> It's easier to bring someone down then pull them up.

> If you want to know what someone is like, look at their friends.

Pretty accurate.

Certain studies indicate that peers and community are more important than family in determining how we turn out.[18]

Estimates say that one out of every four college women are victims of rape or attempted rape.[19] If it's hard to imagine, healthy, middle-class college students turning into arrogant, date-raping, drunk assholes, well, think about the experiment.

this is where

Are men really drunk, date-raping assholes?

Or are men put into environments, much like the fake Stanford prison, where they become such within a few hours?

> Character, then, isn't what we think it is or, rather, what we want it to be. It isn't a stable, easily identifiable set of closely related traits, and it only seems that way because of a glitch in the way our brains are organized. Character is more like a bundle of habits and tendencies and interest, loosely bound together and dependent, at certain times, on circumstance and context. The reason that most of us seem to have a consistent character is that most of us are really good at controlling our environment.[20]

Bad company corrupts good character.

So do bad environments.

There is a story of a man who was working in another man's house.[21] He started out as a pool boy but came to be in charge of the entire house. He was a super pool boy. He was such a great worker that his master trusted everything to him. He was a man of very high character.

The master had a beautiful wife. She was sexy. The pool boy, like all pool boys, was also well built and handsome. And the master's wife wanted to have sex with the pool boy. So, day after day she asked him to come to bed. He refused.

Good character.

One day everyone was gone. They were alone in the house. You can picture it because I'm sure this 2,000-year-old story has been played out on *Desperate Housewives* numerous times. The woman grabs the hot pool boy's shirt, gives him those lustful eyes, and maybe lets her dress slip to reveal a little of that body underneath.

"Come to bed with me now." She nods toward the bedroom and the nice bed that the master has.

The environment has changed and is changing more by the second. What does the servant in the story do?

He runs. He takes off. He flees.

Good character will only take him so far when the environment changes.

> I never thought she would end up with Joe Francis on a bus.
>
> Him? Addicted to porn?
>
> He slept with her?

We're not always as strong as we would like to think.

If you don't want to be a prisoner, get out of the prison.

Control the environment or it may control you.

the couch
The studies keep coming:

> Chethik found that when women are happier with the division of household labors, the couple has a more active sex life. "If men are interested in keeping their sex life vibrant, they may help to wash the dishes and vacuum every now and then."[22]

I used to think the image of the guy sitting on the couch watching a football game with a beer in his hand and asking his wife to bring some pretzels and chips was funny. Then I met those guys. It's not that funny.

Men and lazy have this stereotypical connection. The whole watching sports all weekend, forgetting about the lawn that needs to be mowed, let alone the dishes in the sink and changing the kid's diaper.

If we are lazy, we aren't lazy when we don't want to be. We're lazy when it is convenient. It's not the fact that men won't work hard, it's

this is where

what men will work hard for.

I sometimes wonder why men don't work hard for agape.

We work hard for lots of other things.

>Jobs.
>Cars.
>Boats.
>Trips.
>Sports.
>
>Her? Love?

Agape doesn't expect. It gives.

Have you ever noticed that heroes always seem to be more concerned with giving then getting?

Have you ever noticed that they actually end up getting more than people worried about getting?

Why is that?

a prince
My wife was at Starbucks and while waiting in line saw a newly dating couple. He constantly had his hand on her – her arm, her back – as they walked into the store and then waited in line for their drink.

My wife knew I was writing this book and she called me and said:

> Guys want their wives to act like they did when they were dating – you know, to always want to make-out and to be 'frisky.' The thing is, us girls would like you guys to act the way you did when we dated too. Where are the long gazes, the need for constant touching no matter where we are, and the sweet words that used to always come from your mouth?

My wife's comments were confirmed in a recent report indicating that 40% of women who cheat on their spouses do so because they want more emotional attention.[23] Romance.

A prince and a princess.

If I'm honest, I really don't think medieval princes were that much better than us normal guys in the 21st century. But they did have some things going for them, beyond living in the Middle Ages, being born into royalty, and being rich and upper-class.

There used to be this thing called chivalry. At different times the word meant different things, but most of the time it centered around the knights. The heroes of the day. The guys who hopped on the horses and rode out onto the plains with their shining armor and polished shields fighting the enemy and rescuing the princess.

If you're a man, there's this part of us that always wants to be a knight.

Knights lived by a code. They were dedicated to the virtues of courage, honor, and service.

The code implied courteous behavior toward women: A man had to woo a woman; he had to impress her, respect her, and earn her love and admiration. He had to win her, similar to those whales. I'm not implying that women are little princesses sitting in the castle waiting for their prince to come and rescue them. I am implying that women would love a little courage and honor and service to them.

They would love someone who fights *for* them. They'd love a little chivalry.

When my son was ten he came home from school and told me a conversation he had with his fourth-grade buddies. They were teasing a kid about having a girlfriend and how he was going to kiss her and take off her shirt and bra in her room and be naked with her. They were all hooting and hollering like fourth-graders do, and my son told me that he laughed too but he didn't really like it.

He didn't like it because he knew the girl and is friends with her.

The only thing I could tell my kid was that guys are going to continue to

this is where

talk like that, and talk much worse, and all you need to do is remember to respect women.

A lot of us grow older and still act like fourth graders.

Princely. Above the standard. Holding her in high esteem and acting as though there is nothing better in the world than her happiness.

It was about eight in the morning and me and a friend were waiting for a table at a local diner. A steady rain was coming down outside. As we were standing in the foyer, an older couple appeared. Their hair was as white as snow and they were walking at a turtle's pace. But, they looked sharp. He had on a nice yellow cardigan and she was wearing a flowered dress out of a movie. I couldn't help but think of Marlow and Frances.

They were also holding hands.

Slowly, they made their way past us and out into the rain, together.

We kept watching. The Lincoln Towncar was obviously the one they were headed toward.

They went to her door first. He opened it for her and gently helped her inside before shutting it. And then, ever so slowly, he proceeded around to his door, with the rain still coming down all over his cardigan.

We kept staring, until the car drove away. We then looked at each other and smiled. Topher, the guy I was with, said, "You have to put that into your book."

It was moving. There is no other way to say it.

If you had been standing there with us you would have watched and smiled too.

What was it?

Why do we smile?

What makes us call it beautiful and moving?

THE NAKED FRUIT

Time,
    attention,
        respect,
            sacrifice,
                tenderness,
agape.

It's a wonder the power they have for innocent bystanders, let alone a relationship.

Maybe knights are still around but wearing yellow cardigans now.

Courage, honor, and service. Sweet touches, romance, and chivalry.

Above the standard.

Beautiful.

be it
I remember leaving the movie *300* with some friends and we all wanted to make spears and throw them through the front window of a house or something. We wanted to make love like King Leonidas did with his wife (in slow motion) and with breezes blowing through our thin curtains and blue moonlight reflecting off our body.

We wanted to yell and scream and fight with all of our friends yelling and screaming behind us.

We wanted to do something. Anything. None of us did.

There are a lot of things in life like that. Great to talk and think about but they never really go anywhere.

This shouldn't be one of those.

I could keep writing more. You could keep reading more.

So what?

When are we going to actually do something? Maybe now is the time.

this is where

*Look, there is light,
beauty up there, that no shadow can touch.*

Samwise Gamgee, Return of the King

If we can't live together, we're gonna die alone.

Jack Shephard, Lost

eleven. partners.

The saying goes something like:

> Behind every great man is an even greater woman.

Obviously there are great men and there have been great men throughout history. Behind them are often great women. They could be called greater because they don't get written down in the history books, they don't get the ceremonies and holidays honoring them, and they don't get the statues built to memorialize their deeds.

Yet, they are great human beings, if not greater than the man who gets the attention.

I don't want to write about what women should or shouldn't do, because then it sounds like I know what women should and shouldn't be.

I do want to write about what kind of women men should be looking for to back them up. While men have got to start fighting for this thing, if we don't have someone alongside of us, we're not going to win.

It's just that simple. He needs her.

In the story she got him to eat the fruit. I have little doubt he would have eaten that fruit on his own, eventually. Men will do so much for women that we'll probably even eat bad fruit for them. Sometimes that's not good. But, it can also be the best thing.

What if she had insisted he not eat the fruit?

Women, we need your help.

We need partners here. Partners who are fighting this thing with us. Partners who want something more than mediocre lives.

We need partners who realize that sometimes they are kryptonite and sometimes they are an electronic fence because …

THE NAKED FRUIT

> Sometimes we're superman
>
> and
>
> Sometimes we're a dog in heat

Sometimes a woman is the only thing preventing us from being the hero.

Sometimes a woman is the only thing preventing us from being an idiot.

He needed her.

We need you.

stupid
From what I understand it's fairly hard to accidentally let your garden be visible to all, but two celebrities did that as they were getting in and out of some cars. So, the paparazzi got some nice shots of them to throw all over television and magazines.

That kind of stuff is not really the kind of partners I'm talking about.

We don't need stupid girls (as the singer Pink! describes them).

Stupid girls is not about mental capacity. Stupid girls is not about smarts or math skills. It is about girls who buy into the system that is feeding them lies. It is about them listening to mediocrity and the voices. This is not about laying into women; it is about finding one who will fight for the good with us.

Do you ever ask yourself what happened to the dreams of intelligent, confident girls that don't let men push them around?

Why aren't they all over the news?

Who cares about a geneticist when you can have an anorexic?

It's an epidemic.

partners

The super-model Anna Nicole Smith's death was a tragic story in every way: leaving behind a little baby, men fighting over the baby, strange court procedures, and on and on. However, more sad, in my opinion, is the amount of television coverage that she received after her death. Presidents don't get as much primetime coverage when they are trying to find peace in the Middle East, let alone women who are doing much more for our culture than marrying rich guys and posing nude in magazines.

It's a sickness.

At the time of this writing, the number-one rated show in the 18 to 34 female demographic is *The Girls Next Door*.[1] It's a show about Playboy bunnies, women who live with Hugh Hefner and get naked in front of a camera for a living.

The lies are there for all of us. Men and women.

I'm not a big fan of conspiracy theories. I find most of them pretty funny. But, the more I look around at the world, the more I'm convinced of at least one: I think mediocrity is running things that we think we control.

The world becomes a better breeding ground for the lies every day.

Women are taught things, disguised under words like "famous" and "celebrity" and "sexy" and "cute,' that, in the end, feed men, making us bigger, badder, and more hungry. When we get more hungry, we eat up more girls, we get insatiable desires, and we want women who are raised on the lies.

And on and on it goes.

It's sometimes hard for me to imagine a culture more deceiving than ours, for men and women. It seems like one big setup for us all. It's telling men to get girls to do something and it's telling girls to do whatever it is the men want and in the end none of us are happy with this thing.

Lies are like that though.

Solomon wrote this:

THE NAKED FRUIT

> An excellent wife who can find? …
> Charm is deceptive and beauty is fleeting.[2]

Remember how quiet the truth is? Where is everyone blasting the fact that beauty leaves and charm only goes so far?

What is a man going to be left with when the hot looking, easy-to-manipulate girl, who doesn't think and doesn't zap him when he needs to be zapped, isn't so hot anymore?

If you're a man, don't look for one, and if you're a woman, don't be one.

old school

I was with my 93-year-old grandmother not too long ago. My wife, my kids, and I went and stayed in her house in Philadelphia for a week. She still does the dishes after dinner (if we don't beat her to it) and she still makes dinner (if we don't tell her not to). She's an old-fashioned, strong woman, in every sense of the word.

My grandmom doesn't understand why men change diapers, since her husband never changed them. She comments just about every time she sees me or any of the "new generation" of husbands doing it. It's funny, and we roll our eyes and say, "Grandmom … "

My grandmom and grandpop were married for over 50 years. It's great to sit in my grandmom's living room and talk to her about stuff like love and marriage. She said this when I was with her the last time we visited:

> When your grandfather went to work, he came home tired. I didn't expect him to do anything when he came home. He had been working all day. So, I did the dishes, I did the laundry, I made dinner, I changed the diapers, I scrubbed the floors, and I cleaned the house. I wanted him to come home and relax and I never complained. But, women these days … all they do is bitch and moan about every little bit of work they have to do, and they have it so good. I saw a woman the other day who complained that she couldn't mop the floors because it would mess up her nails, and she had

partners

those long nails that don't let a woman do anything. What's wrong with women these days?

Grandmom ...

My job working on a laptop in a coffee shop and listening to music on my iPhone is not the same job my grandfather did repairing and installing elevators in downtown office buildings in Philadelphia. He came home covered in grease and grime, exhausted, and I come home in flip-flops and full on iced Chai Teas. I'm the first to admit husbands should change diapers and help clean the house.

However, my wife works her butt off and I'm so thankful for it. She works as a mother, works as a business owner, works as a gourmet cook, works as a house cleaner, works as a teacher. If I'm anything close to a great man, it's only because of her.

But there are plenty of men who struggle to be the heroes they could be because their partners are dragging them down. And this is not about the wife doing more. This is not about the husband doing more. This is a partnership – both doing equal, but different, shares.

Solomon wrote more about what he saw as a good partner.

> She looks for wool and flax
> And works with her hands in delight.
>
> She is like merchant ships;
> She brings her food from afar.
>
> She rises also while it is still night
> And gives food to her household
> And portions to her maidens.
>
> She considers a field and buys it;
> From her earnings she plants a vineyard.
>
> She girds herself with strength
> And makes her arms strong.
>
> She senses that her gain is good;

> Her lamp does not go out at night.
>
> She stretches out her hands to the distaff,
> And her hands grasp the spindle.³

In Solomon's lengthy description of a good partner, there was a lot of work involved, rising in the night to take care of her household, planting vineyards, working with her hands, etc.

My grandmom was an amazing wife. She lived very selflessly, dedicated to her husband. She was dedicated to making sure she was everything she could be for her hero. She's still an amazing woman. She still works hard to keep her house in order. She still works hard every morning to be beautiful even though her hero is no longer with her. She still, in the end, just plain works hard, even at ninety-three.

Solomon knew what he was talking about.

partners
If you look up partner in the dictionary, it has a couple of different meanings, one of which is:

> A person with whom one has sex.

Unfortunately, that has become the predominant definition of a partner.

But, the first definition of partner says:

> A person who takes part in an undertaking with another or others, especially in a business or company with shared risks and profits.

That one seems a lot better.

Love is an undertaking. It is a massive task to carry out: fighting lies and eating good fruit. How fulfilling it is to take on that task with a partner, sharing in the risks, of which there are some, and the profits, of which there are many. Profits much better than just "someone to have sex with." Profits that involve the expression and fulfillment of true love. Profits that are unimaginable to those who don't partake or believe in

partners

them. Profits of burning eros flames, friendships that do not waver, and agape-branded soul nourishment.

Heroes, be careful who are you interviewing for your partner. You can't do it alone, and there are plenty of partners that seem good.

Easy. Hot. Charming.

Charm is deceptive and beauty is fleeting.

A woman who will stand beside you and fight with you is worth waiting and searching the world for.

When your parents split up, it's impossible to delude yourself about fairy tale romance and happy endings.

Jennifer Aniston

twelve. happily ever after.

Statistical predictions say that half of all marriages will fail in the United States.[1] That statistic only refers to marriages that "fail" with divorce — not the marriages that fail because no one is actually happy.

We have a better chance of having a marriage that does not bring us any happiness than one that does.

But, no matter the stats, the stories, and the diminishing evidence of anything to the contrary, there is still a belief that happily ever after still exists. And we should believe.

We have to believe beautiful, joyful, precious, delightful, and good still exists.

We have to want the fairy tale.

Some of us *want* the fairy tale but believe the chances are so low of that it's not worth fighting for.

Talk about self-fulfilling.

Some of us *think* that the fairy tale just happens, even if we're married to mediocrity too.

In the end, no matter the reasons, so many of us are missing out. Maybe we settle. Maybe we don't try hard. Maybe we just give up. But, if we don't believe we can have it by fighting a little harder, we won't.

We have to fight for the fairy tale. We have to fight for the agape, the dream, the mango, or whatever else you want to call it.

broken

My wife and I spend quite a bit of time with college students. I have quite a few friends involved on high school campuses across the nation, going to football games, going to basketball games, going to school plays and generally hanging out with "kids."

There has been a common concern between our experiences, our friends' experiences, and many of the articles and news stories I read:

Kids are more broken than ever.

I don't mean "broken" in the way a clock is broken but in the way a heart is broken. They are shattered, fragile, and hurting. They are like those orphans who are never touched. Something has gone wrong in their souls.

I coach football for Jr. High kids. We had a kid on our team who was one of the hardest hitting, toughest, strongest little kids you'll ever meet. He was our stud. He was our Ray Lewis. This kid was an animal. He had our own team scared of him in practice because he would hit so hard.

That was the first year.

The second year, a few games into our season, he was crying. He was begging to come to the sideline. He was giving up at halftime. None of us could figure out what happened. He had always been a nice kid, but his aggressiveness and strength were gone. One day his mom told us she and the kid's dad were getting a divorce and the son was torn up about it. She apologized.

Broken. He could barely make it through a day without crying.

The more I think about it, maybe we are broken in the way a clock is broken: We simply don't function correctly anymore. We can't do what we were made to do. We have a hard time carrying out normal activities or understanding our reason for existence.

Suicide is the third leading cause of death between the ages of 15 to 24.[2]

Beautiful, delightful, joyful, precious and good. You seem so far away.

How many broken kids come from broken families? There seems to be a connection.

The "religious right" espouses the fact that there is a connection with great energy and so I hate to agree with it, because I usually don't agree with the religious right and how they do things. But ... Have you ever met a kid who didn't want his mom and dad to be madly in love with each other?

I once heard a speaker say that three biggest influences on children are their mother, their father, and their mother and father's relationship.

That MTV and Associated Press survey about kids and happiness I mentioned earlier would seem to indicate the same. When asked what makes them happy, the top response was "spending time with family."

In that same study, three-quarters of youths polled indicated that their relationship with their parents makes them happy.[3]

75% of kids said that the relationships with parents made them happy?

What would it look like if 100 percent of marriages succeeded? Not just stayed together in order to say they didn't get a divorce but stayed together because they were built on agape? It's hard to imagine even 60 percent. 40 percent?

It *wants* to happen. It's what we were created to be a part of. It's what we crave. It's how the story began. It's how we are supposed to live and function and there is only one thing in between us and beautiful, delightful, joyful, precious, and good marriages.

Mediocrity is everywhere.

But, what we crave is possible.[4]

promise
G.K. Chesterton wrote this:

> It is the nature of love to bind itself, and the institution of marriage merely paid the average man the compliment of taking him at his word.[5]

I love that. Love *wants* to bind itself. Marriage just allows us the opportunity to do it and mean it.

Not too long ago someone asked me, "Why did you get married?" It took me a minute to think about it, but I think Chesterton was right. I got married because it was what love wanted me to do. Love does desire.

Love wanted me to bind myself to my wife and marriage provided me the opportunity to do it. It's not as though marriage was invented by someone to go against the natural inclination of love; it was institutionalized to allow love to express itself in the way agape wants to.

One could argue that marriage is more natural than sleeping around.

Agape is the driving force, pushing us to get in front of all our family and friends and make promises to those family and friends, and the person we are marrying, and God (if we believe in God) that we will stay together until we die. Unfortunately, there are a lot of people who break all of those promises within two years, and a good 50 years before they die.

I sometimes wonder if anyone would get married with vows like this:

> "Do you promise to love Judy until you are tired of her?"
>
> "Yes, I do."
>
> "Do you promise to love Judy until she gets fat?"
>
> "Yes, I do."
>
> "Do you promise Judy, to love Bob as long as you feel like you did when you were dating and as long as he doesn't want to have too much sex, or at least as long as the sex stays fun?"
>
> "Yes, I do."

Why not? It's what we do.

happily ever after

> If people do not believe in permanent marriage, it is perhaps better that they should live together unmarried than that they should make vows they do not mean to keep.[6]

C.S. Lewis said that; I would have to agree.

Have you been to a wedding where you think "these two are never gonna make it." Have you been to a wedding where you would bet your bank account that "these two are going to make it."

What's the difference? Sometimes you can just feel when a promise is actually a promise. When it's the fulfillment of something real, as though love has awakened and it's palpable between the two making the promise.

And when you are there, isn't it beautiful, good, delightful, precious and joyful? It's as though there is nothing with such a connection to the words as a marriage that means something.

I heard this story at the wedding of some good friends of ours, Ryan and Janny:

It was the night of the bachelor party. The groom and his groomsmen were driving and the best man asked the bachelor to stop his car at the bottom of a big hill. The best man told the groom to get out and push the car up the hill.

He laughed

The best man told him he was serious. So, the groom got out and started pushing.

The car didn't budge.

The best man then got out of the car and started pushing. Soon his other groomsmen got out and strained and fought and pushed until the car was at the top of the hill. The best man told him that there would be some hard times in marriage but he and all the other groomsmen would be there to help him get up whatever hill he came up against.

It's beautiful when you see people understand promises.

By the time we were all dancing to *Celebration* by Kool and the Gang, the excitement in the air was contagious. It was real. Two people committed to being one.

Joyful.

Have you ever watched a 75-year-old couple walk hand in hand, smile at one another and lean in for a kiss?

Precious.

The embodiment of a promise lived.

Delightful.

Promises mean something.

Good.

yum
A couple of years ago a friend of mine was going through a very hard time and standing on the cliff of divorce. He was about ready to take the step off, as was his wife. I remember him saying this, "No one ever told me marriage was hard."

Marriage *is* hard.

At some point we got this idea in our heads that good things aren't hard. I'm not sure why.

Our friends Aaron and Darcy have a great marriage. They are the kind of people who enjoy each other, enjoy marriage, and everything that marriage brings with it. They are sometimes asked what makes their marriage so great and they both respond, "Because we work really hard at it."

People often end marriage because it's hard. You don't just pick up your wife, go to a movie and, after a long make-out session, drop her off at home.

happily ever after

Marriage doesn't work that way.
Sometimes your car breaks.

Sometimes you don't finish the movie because the sitter calls and you have to go home halfway through.

Sometimes you don't get to make-out because you're too tired.

Sometimes she has bad breath and you have body odor and sometimes the kitchen is such a disaster that you need to put away some dishes before you can even get to the bedroom, and by the time you get there no one is in the mood for sex anyway.

Sometimes we get sick and sometimes it just doesn't feel like it used to and sometimes we get so busy we barely see each other and sometimes …

What were you expecting? Easy?

I have a problem with expectations. If someone tells me that a movie was the greatest movie they've ever seen, I will probably hate it. It's hard to meet high expectations.

If they tell me the movie sucks, I'll often like it. It's easy to meet low expectations.

Everyone has expectations for marriage. They are often pretty unrealistic. That's why half of them hate the movie of marriage. The expectation is that it won't take work, that it's easy, that the feelings are never going to end as long as it's "the one."

When there is work, that means it must be over. Right? Nothing beautiful ever takes work?

I'm the kind of guy who likes to get all my work done before I do anything fun. It's just my personality. If there is a game on and I need to mow the lawn, I mow first.

Otherwise I can't enjoy the game, knowing the lawn mower is out there waiting for me. I'll also eat my cooked spinach before I eat the steak, because then I'll really enjoy the steak.

Marriage is kinda like that. Sometimes I have to eat some cooked spinach in my marriage. Sometimes I gag down those parts. I don't give up because I know there is a perfectly cooked filet mignon waiting to dissolve in my mouth and I'll be able to enjoy it so much more when that spinach is gone.

Yum.

I know a couple whose married life wasn't very good for a long time. There were threats of divorce, a couple of "walk-outs" by the wife, but they always came back together and vowed "to stick it out." It's fun to talk to them now. Their kids have left the house and though they have some hard times, they usually say that they are in the best years of their life.

The best years?

Beautiful, why?

They worked.

dead presidents

Per capita income for Americans has doubled in the past forty years, with no measurable increase in individual happiness. Japan's has increased by a factor of five with the same result.[7]

As Barry Schwartz said in his book *The Paradox of Choice*:

> Once a society's level of per capita wealth crosses a threshold from poverty to adequate subsistence, further increases in national wealth have almost no effect on happiness.[8]

If we can buy food, flush the toilet, turn on our heater, watch television, and buy new furniture, why do we argue about money?

Not because we don't have it but because we spend too much of it. The love of money is a root of all sorts of evil.[9]

Shane Claiborne, lives in the slums of North Philly on $150 a month. Shane opens his house to street kids, prostitutes, and whoever else

happily ever after

wants to stop by because he wants to help them. It's good to read about the money he gives away, the little he lives on, and how happy he is.[10]

It's good to read about his time in Calcutta with people who have nothing. Really, nothing. It's good to read about how happy they are with nothing. When I do, it's hard to go argue with my wife about whether or not I can buy the leather couch.

More money will make you have a happy marriage.

Make the lie simple, keep repeating it and eventually they'll believe it.

serve

If you have two people who view their sole purpose in life as making the other person happy, what would that relationship look like?

Compared to ...

Two people who view their sole purpose in life as being happy?

Most relationships end up on a continuum between the two extremes but we can safely say this: The more I care about my spouse's needs and not my own, the better my relationship will be.

I do realize that this isn't always the case. I realize that she can be the greatest, most serving, most not-caring-about-her-own-needs person in the world and her relationship will still suck because he sucks.

I realize that the same thing can happen for him.

However, I also realize that serving is contagious. It feels good and right and beautiful.

I once read on a Starbucks cup ...

> A marriage is only as happy as the least happy person.

What if you always made sure that you were the least happy person?

Mediocrity doesn't like to serve. Mediocrity doesn't like thinking about others. Mediocrity asked her if that fruit was good for *her*. Would it benefit *her*? Why worry about anyone else?

Remember morality? How does she feel? How does he feel?

Think about her. Think about him.

do it
Studies say that 44 percent of men who cheat on their wives, cheat because they want more sex.[11]

I assume Adam wanted to have sex with Eve. I sometimes wonder how often.

We live in a culture of sex. It's everywhere in some form or another. I'm not sure we can even know what natural tendencies are anymore since our environment has changed so much.

He walked around with her naked and he thought, "Hey, it'd be fun to do it right now," because he saw her, he was moved by her, and she was there.

Beautiful.

Men today walk around and see women in lingerie on billboards, they see couples having sex on television and in movies, they hear about people having sex in a good song, and they see women walking down the street wearing tight shirts, and they say, "Hey, it'd be fun to do it," even when their wives are nowhere around.

Beautiful?

There's an obvious difference, a difference that probably leads men to have an unnatural desire. Mediocrity has a done a magnificent job of screwing things up, even our good and natural desires.

Though our desires may have been exaggerated and twisted, I don't think we can argue that they are not important.

Have you ever read about the wedding ceremonies of the ancient

Jews? The party would last for days but before it could really begin, the bride and groom needed to "seal the deal". Remember, the ancient Jews believed that sex was marriage.

It was only after they had sex that they were declared married.

Rob Bell writes,

> Their understanding is that sex is not an optional thing for a marriage, something couples can take or leave. The sexual bond is central to what it means to be married.[12]

Sex is central to what it means to be married. I don't know how often it needs to happen to be central to a marriage but there is no getting around it's importance.

I personally think sex is like oil in an engine: It keeps the marriage running smoothly. If that whole penny in the jar thing is true, that's going to be a rough marriage. If that whole penny in the jar thing isn't true, I would wager it will be a much smoother marriage.

It's funny how often sex resets a marriage. Ask any man, or woman.

As I said earlier, every time we have sex, scientists say that oxytocin is produced and released and oxytocin makes people feel much closer to their partner, assuming there is a healthy relationship.[13]

In marriage relationships that bond is essential to build. So is a healthy relationship.

do it, not that
Sex is not an orgasm. In other words, masturbation is not central to what it means to be married.

Sex is.

In my opinion, frequent masturbation is the cause of a bad sex life as much as it is the result of one.

Masturbation is plan B. I don't want a plan B. When there is a plan B, then plan A suddenly loses it's importance. And if plan A is central to what it means to be married, I don't think we want to lose it.

Authors who argue why masturbation should be a part of relationships say the following.

> It also relieves the pressure for partners to be sexual only together. It provides a sexual outlet for individuals when their partners are disinterested or unavailable.[14]

I'm not sure why the outlet is healthy if the outlet is something other than what it means to be married.

I've seen the results of the relieving of the pressure and I'm not convinced that the pressure should be able to be relieved with your hand.

Masturbation is not exclusive. Although some would argue otherwise, remember that the exclusive we are talking about here is not you, but your spouse. The power and beauty of exclusivity is giving yourself to another person: not giving yourself to your hand while by yourself.

Masturbation is pretty de-motivating. Don't worry, babe, I took care of this one. Why does he or she ever need to take care of the next one?

Masturbation is faux. It's not the real thing. It's not any more real in marriage than it is in dating. It's not the sexual bond that is central to marriage nor does it form any kind of bond beyond you and your hand.

better
When I was in high school I didn't believe people who said, "Sex gets better and better in marriage." It didn't really make sense to me. What thing gets better and better the more you do it? There aren't many, if any, that I can think of. Even eating. That's why we go to new restaurants and try new recipes. Most things get worse the more you do them because we get bored pretty easily and we eventually don't find the appeal in something we have done hundreds of times.

If it gets better that generally means that it has to be changing. Sure, there are some new positions, new environments, and a random crazy twist here and there, but if we're honest, sex is, for the most part in a monogamous relationship, the same thing every time.

Yet, it *does* get better. How?

Maybe the kind of sex we're talking about isn't just an act between two bodies, but the result of lots of acts between two people. It's always transforming and evolving.

It's not just physical, it's spiritual. It's connecting. It's mystical and deep. It's relationship.

Things don't stay stagnant in a relationship. They change. They move. They grow.

And as a result, so does the sex. Sex that changes and grows and gets better?

Sex as the result of something instead of trying to make something happen.

And we really convince ourselves we want Cancun sometimes?

If it's not getting better what does that mean?

unite
I was with a group of people who asked me what the best thing about marriage is. Being a man, my first answer was sex. That was just to be funny ... I think.

I wonder if sex comes to mind for a reason. It's the best indicator of what I truly think is the coolest thing about marriage: being one with another person.

Adam said Eve was flesh of his flesh. Bone of his bone. He indicated that they were one. They were one physically, mentally, emotionally, and spiritually. They connected. And I'm not sure there is anything better in a relationship than being connected, and growing more connected in every form, with another person.

In fact, it's beyond good; it's amazing. It's miraculous. There is no other relationship like it in the world. It's what we all crave. It's what we seek.

THE NAKED FRUIT

It's not sex. It's not conversation. It's not sleeping in the same bed. It's not having kids. It's not saying vows.

It is being united together. It is becoming a single new organism, binding to one another and leaving the old desires and wants and needs behind. It is as mysterious as anything on earth: words, promises, and a ceremony that join two souls together into one.

It's unbelievably beautiful. It's raw delight. Precious, joyful, and good.

Promises.
Work.
Serving.
Friendship.
Sex.

Think about it. Really think.

Think about what you did at that altar or what you hope to do some day. Think about two people becoming one. Joining their thoughts, their dreams, their passions, their priorities, their minds, their emotions, their bodies, and their souls into something new, together, as a unified creation.

That is an amazing fruit.

I'd say it's a beautiful, joyful, delightful, precious and good fruit.

A damn good fruit.

happily ever after

A single idea from the human mind can build cities. An idea can transform the world and rewrite all the rules.

Cobb, Inception

*God forbid that Achilles sees me turning tail,
Heading from town and out to open country –
He'll come after me full tilt and run me down!
And then no way to escape my death, my certain doom –
Achilles is far too strong for any man on earth.
Wait ... what if I face him out before the walls?
Surely his body can be pierced by bronze, even his –
He has only one life, and people say he's mortal:*

Homer's Iliad

thirteen. the soul of the matter.

There is something else going on here, right? Good sex is soul sex. Bad sex harms something deep, something in the heart of who we are: where the soul resides.

This whole movement, these fruits – they seem to have a lot more to do with the soul than anything else. If that's true, this battle is being fought much deeper, well below the surface. This is more than just pornography, strip clubs and masturbation. Those are just the little bubbles that make their way up.

If that's true, than mediocrity is really, at the end of the day, probably more concerned about this soul stuff than anything. At the end of the day, mediocrity is fighting this war where the soul resides, because if he changes the soul, he changes everything.

I wonder if all mediocrity has ever been truly concerned with, is the soul.

That was all he was after in the beginning, in that first story, and it's all he's after still in our story. Maybe because it's in the soul where that nasty smelling smoke of evil really sinks in.

Maybe because it's in the soul where beauty, delight, precious, joy, and good truly live or truly die.

good news

> If we did all that Plato or Aristotle or Confucius told us, we should get on a great deal better than we do. And so what? We never have followed the advice of the great teachers. Why are we likely to begin now? ... There has been no lack of good advice for the last four thousand years. A bit more makes no difference.[1]

I'm a Christian.

I'm a Christian for the following reasons: beautiful, delightful, joyful, precious and good.

Those words represent what I believe Christianity truly is.

Those words are how this book started.
They are how this book is ending.

Those words are how the Christian story started.
They are how the Christian story ends.

Christianity is about reminding us of some very good news – the news that the story started out with beautiful and it ends with beautiful and though we don't see it in a lot of places anymore, we can bring some of it back in the middle of the story.

I like that.

Christianity is not more rules and guidelines. That's just another religion. We already, as C.S. Lewis said, have more than enough rules we're not following.

Christianity is about something deeper.

Remember the story about the man who was told to keep loving the woman who slept with other men? Remember the story of the man who was supposed to keep loving the prostitute? That story is meant to represent God's love for me and for you. God said this to the husband in the story.

> Go, show your love to your wife again, though she is loved by another and is an adulteress. Love her as the Lord loves the Israelites … [2]

The Israelites were God's people in the story. He used the analogy of marriage. God used the analogy of a lover cheating on her beloved to represent the way it is when humans love other things more than God. To represent the way it is when humans listen to mediocrity and when they believe the lies. To represent falling in love with Mediocrity more than Beautiful.

To represent the way it is when we leave God's original intention for us:

beautiful, joyful, delightful, precious and good.

Toward the end of the story, God says:

> My heart is changed within me;
> all my compassion is aroused.
> I will not carry out my fierce anger,
> nor will I turn and devastate Ephraim.
> For I am God, and not man—
> the Holy One among you.
> I will not come in wrath.[3]

I will not come in wrath. That's pretty amazing.

I'm as angry and as jealous as any lover would be. But, my greatest concern and sorrow and motivation is to show you beautiful, delightful, joyful, precious and good.

This God says that's what I'm about. I want that for you, for us, for him and her more than anything. I want to know you and show you more of this beautiful, delightful, joyful, precious and good in your life.

Christianity is best represented by Jesus.

Jesus was a man who walked on this Earth and said that if you have seen me, you've seen God.[4]

In other words, if you're interested in what God looks like, in how much God wants beauty, delight, joy, precious, and good, look at me, Jesus said.

It *isn't* always easy. In fact, Jesus was tortured and killed.

It *isn't* always about being in charge. In fact, Jesus lived to serve … even enemies.

It *isn't* always about being right and religious. In fact, Jesus had harsh things to say to you if you thought you were.[5]

It *is* about life. In fact, Jesus came back from the dead to bring life.

THE NAKED FRUIT

It *is* about fruit, which is where this whole story started. Jesus talked about fruit quite a bit. He said you can tell a good tree by the fruit it produces in the same way you can tell a bad tree by the fruit it produces.[6]

Those fruits are about love, grace, compassion, healing, and beauty, delight, joy, precious, and good.

It *is* about a piece of us dying to being in charge and to being right and religious in order that we might have life and grace and compassion and healing and beauty and delight and joy with something precious and good.

It *is* about our souls becoming something different than they were and knowing the original creator of good, beauty, delight, joy, and precious in the way a bride knows her husband: intimately.

It *is* about cleaning out the nasty furniture in our house and making it smell good again.

I like that. I believe God likes that even more.

I think Jesus came to say how much God likes that.

As Huston Smith put it:

> Instead of telling people what to do or what to believe, he [Jesus] invited them to see things differently, confident that if they did so their behavior would change. This called for working with people's imagination more than with their reason or their will.[7]

So, Christianity becomes something more than rules and guidelines. It becomes a source of power and change and movement toward beautiful, delightful, joyful, precious and good.

Christianity is not willing myself to not look at porn because it's wrong. It's not me staring at the video and arguing with the demon on my shoulder who is pushing my hand toward it while I resist and try to pull my hand away with sweat dripping off my forehead and my arms shaking.

the soul of the matter

Christianity is removing the *desire* to look at porn because it's not beautiful and I don't want things that aren't beautiful.

Christianity is not convincing myself that it's good to serve my wife. It's about making it my natural inclination for me to serve my wife because it delights her.

Christianity is about transforming people through their souls because this whole battle starts there anyway.

It's about letting God move us.

Christianity is not about making myself follow rules, it's about wanting to live a way that brings beauty, delight, joy, precious and good back to our world. If some rules do that, so be it. This is about much more than rules. Rules become pathways to beauty and a transformed soul craves more of that beauty for this world.

Christianity is about becoming a different person, really. A new person. A transformed person.[8]

I'm not so sure that mediocrity is afraid of some rules and guidelines. I'm pretty sure he despises new people who have tasted beauty and want more of it.

I'm pretty sure mediocrity cringes and screams at transformed, new, creations.

They, hurt him where it hurts the most.

They have the power to kill him.

And that is why anything that does not affect the soul, may weaken mediocrity, may make things better for a moment, but will never work in the long run.

This soul thing more than matters. It's everything.

You have the freedom to choose your actions; you don't have the freedom to choose the consequences of your actions.

Anonymous

fourteen. endings.

bleeding
Beautiful. Delightful. Joyful. Precious. Good

Let's say you haven't lived it. You've made mistakes. You've messed up.

What now? Is there any chance to get it back?

Yes. That's the good news. If there wasn't we would all be in a lot of trouble.

First, the bad news.

There is no starting over. I know too many people who live with consequences that haven't gone away: psychological, physical and emotional.

I know too many people who still have the scars from wounds received years earlier. They have recovered but they spent many years dealing with the wounds, and the scars still trouble them from time to time.

I wrote this book because I don't like the wounds and the scars. I want fewer people walking around with them. The only way to have fewer wounds is to make decisions that don't give them to us in the first place.

There's no other way.

There are consequences to our actions. I've seen them. You've seen them.

Mediocrity won't be denied his damage.

That's the bad news. But listen closely. None of this means we should throw in the towel.

THE NAKED FRUIT

I've already screwed up. What's the point in …

I've already lost my virginity to him. I may as well …

I've already looked at porn. There's nothing I can …

I've already been to a strip club …

I've already been to Cancun …

I've already ruined a marriage …

I've already …

No you haven't. It's not true. It's not beautiful, delightful, joyful, precious, or good and it's certainly no way to turn the ship around and start down the path that is.

Don't let your mind go there. Mediocrity would love nothing better than for you to. It's the path that leads to more destruction and chaos than there already is.

Picture yourself chopping some veggies with a sharp knife. The knife slips and gives you a good gash on the finger. It's bleeding everywhere.

You're going to have a scar.

The best advice is not to pick up the knife and cut your finger again.

And again.

And again.

And then cut your arms and then your legs and then your face until you can hardly walk or function.

The best advice is to put the knife down and get a Band-Aid: to do something to stop the bleeding. That doesn't mean that the wound will instantly go away or that there won't be a scar even after it heals.

However, it does end the damage. It does limit the healing time and the

endings

scar to a small one on your finger.

Our sexual decisions leave scars. That "sword" Solomon described cuts every time.

Every time. No matter whether it's your first time or your hundredth time, it's another slice. Some are bigger than others, but they each bleed and take time to heal. There are lots of people who keep cutting themselves because they have a small gash on their finger, and they think once they have one cut the damage can't get any worse.[1]

It's not true.

If you have a couple of scars or some cuts on your hand, put down the knife. Don't keep going for bigger, more visible or damaging cuts. Remember the stripper: Her wounds are deep and they are not healing easily. It will take time and work, sometimes years and sometimes painstaking effort.

Remember the man who left his wife and kids because of a porn addiction: He kept cutting himself and his wounds became so deep that he lost everything.

It doesn't matter what we've already done: Not because there aren't any scars or wounds, but because we can't go back and change any of it. We're going to have to deal with those decisions one way or another.

That's the bad news.

Here's the good news.

I believe there is a God who loves nothing more than healing wounds and transforming their damage into something beautiful, joyful, precious, delightful, and good.

I believe we are offered a peace that exceeds anything we can understand.[2] A peace that doesn't make sense. A peace that will turn us around and start to bring healing: beautiful, joyful, precious, delightful, good healing.

The wounds can heal. Believe they can.

This isn't the part of the book where I say that everything will be great if you've screwed up –at least not quickly and easily, especially if you have some slices that go deep.

But, no matter where you are, know this:

Today it can start getting more beautiful. That's great news and reason to start making different decisions. Today you can start down a road of more delight. More joy. More precious. More good.

Today it can start getting worse. That's not-so-great news but an equally good reason to start making different decisions.

You have to believe both are possible and in your hands. You haven't hit bottom and there is still time to move one direction or the other. No matter where you're at, no matter what you've done, no matter your history, there are new choices today that will determine your future.

versus
I was in Seattle with my wife to hear Rob Bell speak. Before the "show" we were doing some shopping, and I came across the book entitled *I Hope They Serve Beer in Hell*.

Here is what the back of the book says:

> My name is Tucker Max and I am an asshole. I get excessively drunk at inappropriate times, disregard social norms, indulge every whim, ignore the consequences of my actions, mock idiots and posers, sleep with more women than is safe or reasonable, and just generally act like a raging dickhead. But I do contribute to humanity in one very important way. I share my adventures with the world.[3]

A couple of hours later, Rob Bell shared a story about a woman who was in a car accident. Her face was damaged severely and she had to undergo major surgery to try and reconstruct it. The doctor was unable to fix her mouth very well – the best he could do was give her a crooked smile. Regardless, at the unveiling of her face (the first time anyone

endings

had seen the results of the accident and subsequent surgeries), her husband stood by her bed. As the face wrapping came off to reveal the changed face of his wife, the husband immediately bent over, kissed her crooked smile and said, with a romantic tone, "I like it."

The Tipping Point, which talks about how trends catch on and things become popular, makes a key point: It only takes a few critical people to start a fire.[4]

It only takes a few critical people to start a fad, to start an epidemic, to create a phenomenon, to start people thinking and changing.

We are where we started. Him and her.

Men and women.

Mediocrity is whispering in our garden. In our world. In your world.

He's asking questions about fruit. In fact, they are both right there, staring at you. No matter where you've been, they are hanging there right now, staring at you.

> I generally act like a raging dickhead.
>
> and
>
> I like it.

The whispers are everywhere. The lies are repeating. The truth is quiet.

Beauty, delight, joy, precious, and good for you, and the rest of us, are in the balance.

What will you do?[5]

*Express your gratitude.
Give credit when it's due - and even when it isn't.*

gratitude. endnotes.

thank you to.

all of the following friends for reading the book in one of its various stages and giving me feedback: The Donut Boys (Chad D, Matt K, and Tom D), Dave S, Leslie D, Emily, Rob F, Russ and Shannon D, Linda, Kent and Lauren M, Summer C, Chris M, Ryan W, Daryl J, Ryan and Janny K, Nick K, and Topher W.

for editing: Lynn S.

for agent stuff (we will make this happen eventually): Christi C.

helping me write this thing, in so many ways: my wife, Heidi.

And to all the authors of various books, articles, and anything else listed below ...

one.

1 The headline said on the article said it all: "Elizabeth Smart Says She Was Raped Daily" (http://abcnews.go.com/US/wireStory?id=8722737)

2 On that day, it so happen that right alongside that story was "Schwarzenegger Asked To Close Prostitute Website" (http://www.reuters.com/article/idUSTRE5905CU20091001)

3 "Welcome to PunterNet! You have reached the premier site for Adult Service Provider (Escorts, Massage, and all other Working Ladies) Reviews and Listings in the UK" (http://www.punternet.com)

4 "Mathematicians Figure Out What Makes Women Beautiful" I think we were all okay before mathematicians figured it out but oh well... (http://gizmodo.com/gadgets/babes/mathemeticians-figure-out-what-makes-women-beautiful-293838.php)

two.

1 Oprah.com has a summary of the episode along with some clips. (http://www.oprah.com/oprahshow/Boys-Will-Be-Boys)

2 The video is on the Mayo Clinic website and, yes, it's classic. (http://sharing.mayoclinic.org/2009/05/25/mayo-clinic-octogenarian-idols-good-morning-america/)

3 You can read all about the poll on the Washington Post, along with lots of other sites. Some very interesting stuff. (http://www.washingtonpost.com/wp-dyn/content/article/2007/08/20/AR2007082000451.html)

4 Seth Godin is one of my favorite authors. I tried to get into his class in New York City but was denied. I still love him. If you want to read a great book check out *Linchpin: Are You Indispensable?* (New York,NY: Portfolio, 2010) page 25 (to be exact)

5 Bradley Gerstman, Christopher Pizzo, and Rich Seldes M.D., will tell you *What Men Want* (New York, NY: Harper-Collins Publishers, Inc., 2000) in their book including the desire for variety on page 144. But, I'll let you in on a secret – they basically want sex.

6 Jonah Lehrer is another amazing writer. His blog (http://scienceblogs.com/cortex/) The Frontal Cortex is also one of my favorites. For a look at how the brain works and how we make decisions, check out How We Decide (New York, NY: Houghton Miffin Co., 2009) p. 87

7 The video is called "Amsterdam: Red Light District." and was talked about in a xxxchurch.com podcast on February 20, 2006.

three.

1 Not sure a survey was really needed for that statistic but in case it was ABC News was on the case... "American Sex Survey: A Peek Beneath the Sheets." 21 October 2004. (http://abcnews.go.com/Primetime/News/story?id=156921&page=1)

2 Further proof that pastors are just people who happen to speak at churches. I think I still want them to be something more. "How Many Porn Addicts are in Your Church?" (http://www.crosswalk.com/1336107/)

3 You ever wonder who takes in the most of that 5 billion? I don't know. (http://en.allexperts.com/e/s/st/strip_club.htm)

4 The article was called "Six Ways that Porn Runs the World." by Ian Cheesman from April 30, 2009. (http://www.cracked.com/article_17300_p2.html) When you start throwing out numbers like that, it's safe to say that porn does, in many ways, run the world.

5 There are lots more pornography statistics at this site (http://www.familysafemedia.com/pornography_statistics.html) including things like every 39 minutes a new porn video is being created in the United States and every second over 28,000 people are looking at pornography.

6 Quite a few people say it but one is Willard F. Harley Jr. in *His Needs, Her Needs: Building an Affair Proof Marriage* (Grand Rapids, MI, Baker Book House Co., 2005) on page 59.

7 We always want/need something to fight don't we? Just take a day to listen to progressive talk radio and conservative talk radio. They will both bash the mainstream media's attempts to not tell the truth about their side. They will both call out the devil. It's interesting to even look at the green movement or the "buy local" movement. Of course, it benefits our health and our planet but it's amazing how much more passionate we become about it when we are doing it to fight the evil companies making money off of the planet or the corporations selling us cheap food. Brian McLaren makes the statement about devils and dives in a bit more in his tremendous book called *A New Kind of Christianity: Ten Questions That Are Transforming the Faith* (New York, NY: HarperCollins, 2010) page 175.

8 Just for the record, I'm still not sure how or why women want to live with Hugh Hefner and have sex with the man that makes money off of taking pictures of them, but I guess that's not the point.

9 And suddenly so many things make sense. Thanks Jonah Lehrer. *How We Decide* (New York, NY: Houghton Miffin Co., 2009) page 114.

10 Joe Wittwer is a pastor at LifeCenter Church in Spokane, Washington. Good pastor, good man, and good friend. Actually he's not a friend but it sounded better and I have met him.

11 Sexting. Not something I dealt with in High School. (http://www.capecodonline.com/apps/pbcs.dll/article?AID=/20090211/NEWS/902110317)

12 That may not sound like too much - how does 14 minutes a day sound? (http://www.dailymail.co.uk/sciencetech/article-1139811/Teens-spend-average-87-hours-year-looking-porn-online.html)

13 Why wouldn't they think that? (http://www.capecodonline.com/apps/pbcs.dll/article?AID=/20090211/NEWS/902110317)

14 I don't look at Playboy, even for the interviews. But I did look at it for this interview from March 2010. It sure makes me think about things differently now when I hear "Your Body is a Wonderland" now. (http://www.playboy.com/articles/john-mayer-playboy-interview/index.html)

15 That would be Tom Leykis.

16 Really Tucker Max? Do you really mean that? *I Hope They Serve Beer in Hell* (New

gratitude

York, NY: Citadel Press Books, 2006, 2008) page 91.

17 C.S. Lewis is one of my favorites and the best to ever write... and think. *The Four Loves* (Orlando, FL: Harcourt Brace & Company, 1960) page 94.

18 Only Lewis can describe hormones poetically. *Surprised By Joy: The Shape of My Early Life* (Orlando, FL: Harcourt Brace & Company, 1955) page 69.

19 This CNN story, by Arwa Damon from August 2007, was one of those that put a pit in my stomach. A part of the war that we don't think about too much. "Iraqi Women: Prostituting Ourselves to Feed Our Children." (http://www.cnn.com/2007/WORLD/meast/08/15/iraq.prostitution/index.html)

20 The blog The Cunning Realist posted some hi-lights from the "International Sex Guide": a website that features reviews on prostitutes from around the world. The reviews I quote came from the section on Iraq. (http://cunningrealist.blogspot.com/2007/08/this-thing.html)

21 Peter tweeted this not too long ago. But if you want more than a tweet, read his amazing book How (Not) to Speak of God (London, UK: Paraclete Press, 2006)

four.

1 And it was probably a lot more poetic in the original Hebrew. A lot more. Genesis 2:23

2 Tom Leykis makes a living on crossing the line, but still.... (http://www.blowmeuptom.com/leykis-or-not/comments.php?DiscussionID=17&page=1%06)

3 Not sure what American men would say but I have no reason to believe it would be much different. Scary. (http://www.womanabuseprevention.com/html/sexual_assault.html)

4 There are quite a few studies on assaults and rapes on college campuses and none of them are super uplifting. (http://collegeuniversity.suite101.com/article.cfm/college_students_sexual_violence)

5 The point of this article on MSNBC was how diet can affect our sex life. I couldn't get past the sexless marriage statistic. (http://www. msnbc.msn.com/id/23018588/)

6 That same poll. Lots of goodies in there. (http://www.washingtonpost.com/wp-dyn/content/article/2007/08/20/AR2007082000451.html)

7 If you want to learn that you aren't nearly as smart as you think and that, in fact, you are persuaded to do things you probably don't want to do every day, read Dr. Robert Cialidini's book *Influence: The Psychology of Persuasion* (New York, NY: William Morrow and Company: 1993) This quote comes from page 17 but in it you'll learn why you bought the shirt, why you donated money, and, most importantly, how to recognize the triggers that marketers, lovers, and lots of other people are using on you.

8 Ibid. Dr. Cialdini says how we should react to the salesperson who gives us a sample to try in order to get us to buy something: "the reciprocity rule asserts that if justice is to be done, exploitation attempts should be exploited." Exploit them back.

9 Still quoting that powerful book. Ibid. page 57.

10 A NY Times article by Jane Perlez going into more detail. Hard stuff. (http://www.nytimes.com/1996/03/25/world/romanian-orphans-prisoners-of-their-cribs.html?sec=health)

11 Yep parents do matter. A lot. Whitehead, Barbara Dafoe. "Facing the Challenges of Fragmented Families."The Philanthropy Roundtable 9.1 (1995): 21.

12 Hugh MacLeod's amazing book is called *Ignore Everybody And 39 Other Keys to Creativity* (New York, NY, The Penguin Group, 2009) You'll read it and be inspired to do something. Anything. This quote is page 110.

13 You can see the ads yourself at adgoodnesss.com (http://www.frederiksamuel.com/blog/2007/03/polaroid-eyewear.html)

14 Funny I have seen this show once and this was the episode my wife and I watched. I went straight to the internet to try and find the quotes and was able to on IMDB. Ah, the internet. (http://www.imdb.com/title/tt0549667/quotes)

15 Of course I loved the movies. Yes, I loved the books more. Not sure if this line was in the books or not, but it was in the first movie, and it was a great line.

***

1 The recent "Life" series from the BBC has some amazing footage of these fights as well as a male and female heading down into the depths of the ocean to supposedly mate. If you haven't seen Life, go buy it.

2 Lots of little goodies in this very interesting read by Robert Wright, *The Moral Animal. Why We Are, the Way We Are: The New Science of Evolutionary Psychology* (New York, NY: Vintage Books, 1994) page 46.

3 This book was a big one for men a few years back and got lots of men amped up about being men. Not sure if I was that man but I appreciated a lot about that book from John Eldredge. *Wild at Heart: Discovering the Secret of a Man's Soul* (Nashville, TN: Thomas Nelson, 2001) page 9.

4 From what I've seen, it must be hard to actually determine whether or not men or women speak more. Dr. Louann Brizendine talks about that (and other probably more important matters) in The Female Brain (New York, NY: Broadway Books, 2006) The stat I used was on page 26.

5 The title of this one pretty much says it all. "Science proves it: Men talk as much as women, if you just round the numbers" (http://www2.canada.com/montrealgazette/news/arts/story.html?id=2ed2cd3b-58f5-420a-a10a-0edbb0fd0d6e)

6 Another great article title: "MTV survey says boys think sexting is hot, girls think it's slutty, and a third of you have done it" (http://www.intomobile.com/2009/12/03/mtv-survey-says-boys-think-sexting-is-hot-girls-think-its-slutty-and-a-third-of-you-have-done-it.html)

7 Apparently there are experts on virginity, not because they are virgins but because the have studied virginity. Hanne Blank is one and she is interviewed in this article. (http://www.scarleteen.com/article/politics/20_questions_about_virginity_scarleteen_interviews_hanne_blank)

8 I highly doubt this desire is limited to Indian men. (http://www.alertnet.org/thenews/newsdesk/DEL8022.htm)

9 "Every Woman Has Five Reasons to Recover Her Virginity." Once again, the title alone says a lot. (http://english.pravda.ru/print/science/health/99808-virginity-0)

10 I'm not sure how this story ever ended. I hope he got his money worth. I do know most people get zero dollars for their virginity. (http://www.cnn.com/2009/LIVING/01/22/virginity.value/index.html)

11 Rob Bell is one of my favorite authors, favorite speakers and favorite thinkers. I'm not alone. His book *Sex God: Exploring the Endless Connections between Sexuality and Spirituality* (Grand Rapids, MI: Zondervan, 2007) is amazing. The quote is on page 139.

12 If you have never read the Dilbert Blog, you should. Scott Adams is a genius. (http://dilbertblog.typepad.com/the_dilbert_blog/2007/05/footwear_theory.html)

13 Amazing how much you can learn about a society via Google searches. (http://trueslant.com/erikkain/2010/01/12/google-sex-and-matrimonial-bliss/)

14 I mentioned The International Sex Guide earlier. (http://www.internationalsexguide.info/) I really don't recommend "checking out" this site unless you can come up with some benefit to reading the exploits of these guys. I can't.

15 Sad stuff. (http://www.eyewitnesstohistory.com/rommel.htm).

16 A condom maker carried out the study. (http://sev.prnewswire.com/retail/20090701/

gratitude

NY4086801072009-1.html)

17 Another one of those books that will inspire you, make you think, and open your eyes. Steven Pressfield, *The War of Art: Break Through the Blocks and Win Your Inner Creative Battles* (New York, NY: Warner Books, 2002) page 54.

six.

1 I'm not trying to be dramatic here but I've numerous people tell me the warning should, at least, be here. So, reminds me a little of Aragorn and Frodo when they are at the Inn of the Prancing Pony in *The Fellowship of the Ring*. Aragorn says to Frodo, "Are you afraid?" Frodo answers, "Yes." Aragorn returns, "Not nearly enough." Maybe some of us just aren't afraid enough.

2 Hard to believe that for every 4 girls you see on a high school campus, 1 of them has an STD. (http://www.msnbc.msn.com/id/23574940/)

3 "Children Say Being Famous is Best Thing in World." (http://www.independent.co.uk/news/uk/this-britain/children-say-being-famous-is-best-thing-in-world-429000.html)

4 Steven Pressfield again in *The War of Art: Break Through the Blocks and Win Your Inner Creative Battles* (New York, NY: Warner Books, 2002) page 54.

5 Because sex in a dirty bar bathroom is so hot. (http://www.frederiksamuel.com/blog/SINGLE_AD_PAGE.php?ad=axe_bathroom.jpg)

6 You can check out the ad yourself, if you haven't seen it already. And if you want to. (https://www.cpyu.org/widgets/download.aspx?file=%2ffiles%2fCurrent+Culture+Image%2f2009%2f1st+Quarter%2fAxe+2-11-2009+hires.jpg)

7 The list is compiled from a couple books including Steve Santagi's *The Manual: A True Bad Boy Explains How Men Think, Date, and Mate – and What Women Can Do to Come Out on Top* (New York, NY: Crown, 2007) and Bradley Gerstman, Christopher Pizzo, and Rich Seldes' What Men Want (New York, NY: HarperCollins, 2000).

8 C.S. Lewis actually received quite a bit on criticism for writing this book: for entering into the mind of the devil. I'm glad he did it. *The Screwtape Letters* (New York, NY: HarperCollins, 1996) page 107.

9 Every time I read this article from Claire Hoffman I get a pit in my stomach. LA Times.com. August 2006 (http://articles.latimes.com/2006/aug/06/magazine/tm-gonewild32)

10 Abby Lee has written a book and continues on with her sex blog. (http://girlwithaonetrackmind.blogspot.com/2007/03/hotel-ii.html)

11 A powerful video podcast from xxxchurch.com released on the 21st of February 2006.

12 The stories are everywhere. (http://www.academicleadership.org/emprical_research/572.shtml)

13 Lots of porn statistics all in a single little chart. (http://gizmodo.com/5552899/finally-some-actual-stats-on-internet-porn)

14 Watch the movie Trade if you haven't seen it. (http://abcnews.go.com/Primetime/story?id=1596778&page=1)

15 Gut wrenching stuff by Victor Malarek *The Natashas: Inside the New Global Sex Trade* (New York, NY: Arcade, 2003) page 33.

16 (http://www.darkness2light.org/KnowAbout/statistics_2.asp)

17 You can see their happy faces if you want to. (http://www.techcrunch.com/2009/02/03/thousands-of-myspace-sex-offender-refugees-found-on-facebook)

18 The same porn statistics chart again. (http://gizmodo.com/5552899/finally-some-actual-stats-on-internet-porn)

19 Another powerful podcast from xxxchurch.com. They have lots of them. This one is

from October 1, 2007.

20 P.J Huffstutter wrote the powerful article "See No Evil" in January 2003 for the Los Angeles Times. (http://articles.latimes.com/2003/jan/12/magazine/tm-porn)

21 "Pornmobile Confessions Episode Number 2: 'Luke.' " August, 13 2007 from xxxchurch.com

22 "Number of Unwed Mothers Has Risen Sharply in U.S." by Rob Stein and Donna St. George for The Washington Post.com. 14 May 2009. (http://www.washingtonpost.com/wp-dyn/content/article/2009/05/13/AR2009051301628.html?hpid=topnews)

23 Anthony DeMello, *The Way To Love* (New York, NY: Image Books, Doubleday, 1995) page 01. Amazing little book. Absolutely amazing. And really little.

24 Fyodor Dostoevsky. *The Best Short Stories of Fyodor Dostoevsky The Ridiculous Man*. (New York: Modern Library, 2001) page 277.

25 "Condom Nations" by Miguel Fontes and Peter Roach. September/October 2007 (http://www.foreignpolicy.com/story/cms.php?story_id=3933)

26 The chart one more time. (http://gizmodo.com/5552899/finally-some-actual-stats-on-internet-porn)

27 I first heard of David Mura in David Foster Wallace's book, *Consider the Lobster* in his powerful first chapter on the porn industry's award show in Las Vegas. David Mura. *A Male Grief: Notes on Pornography and Addiction* (Minneapolis, MN Milkweed Editions, 1987)

seven.

1 Daniel Goleman Social Intelligence (New York, NY: Bantam, 2006) pages 189-193.

2 This is by no means the end all be all on love. In fact, if you want to read an entire book on the different aspects of love, I recommend The Four Loves by C.S. Lewis, who also bases it off of the Greek.

3 "Truly, Madly, Guiltily" by Ayelet Waldman in the New York Times.com, March 27, 2005 (http://www.nytimes.com/2005/03/27/fashion/27love.html?)

4 Stephanie Meyers *Twilight: The Twilight Saga* (New Yor, NY: Time Warner Book Group, 2005) page 276.

5 Book of Hosea in the Old Testament. Weird book. If you don't believe me, read it.

6 Hosea 3:3

7 I just watched *Amelie* again. Great film. Love it. But, after two hours of amazing storytelling, this beautiful love story ends with Amelie having sex with a guy minutes after their first real encounter. It made me think how integrated this idea of eros is in our culture. It's how a great love story even ends, as though that is the indicator of love. Of course, *Amelie* isn't the only movie with the same story.

8 Thank you again C.S. Lewis. *The Screwtape Letters* (New York, NY: HarperCollins, 1996) page 97.

9 St. John Chrysostom was called "The Golden Mouth" and if you read some of the things he said, you realize why. *On Marriage and Family Life* (Crestwood, NY: St. Vladimir's Seminary Press, 1986) page 100

eight.

1 Who knew Banana's changed the world? Dan Koeppel does because he wrote the book Banana: The Fate of the Fruit that Changed the World (New York, NY: Hudson Street Press, 2008) page x.

2 Chip Heath and Dan Heath in their book *Switch: How to Change Things When Change is Hard* (New York, NY: Broadway Books, 2010) talk about teaching monkeys to skateboard on page 251. How were they taught? Not with punishment but reward - they

gratitude

were given some mango each time they did something right. They also talk about Amy Sutherland's attempts to do the same thing to her husband. Great stuff.

3 Jane Weaver writes for MSNBC on who is cheating and why. April 16, 2007. (http://www.msnbc.msn.com/id/17951664/ns/health-sexual_health/)

4 Another genius is Frederick Buechner. *Wishful Thinking* (New York, NY: Harper Collins, 1993) page 87

5 I think there was a good motive to writing about the "rule". But I'm still not sure I buy it. Stephen Arterburn, Fred Stoeker and Mike Yorkey wrote *Every Man's Marriage: An Every Man's Guide to Winning the Heart of a Woman* (Colorado Springs, CO: WaterBrook Press, 2001) p. 244

6 I got to hear Shane Claiborne speak at Whitworth University in February 2007. It was a treat.

7 I really liked parts of Greg Behrendt and Liz Tuccillo's *He's Just Not That Into You: The No-Excuses Truth to Understanding Guys* (New York, NY: Simon Spotlight Entertainment, 2004) But if a woman has to read that line on page 47 and that a man who is married, a man who has sex with other people and a man who only likes a woman when he is drunk isn't "into you", I'm very scared.

8 Steve Santagi, *The Manual: A True Bad Boy Explains How Men Think, Date, and Mate--and What Women Can Do to Come Out on Top* (New York, NY: Crown Publishing, 2007)

9 Check out Song of Solomon some time. You might be surprised. Chapter 2:3

10 Song of Solomon 4:16

11 Song of Solomon 7:7

12 Song of Solomon 8:12

13 Song of Solomon 2:7, 3:5, and 8:4

14 Thank you for enlightening me to vasopressin Joe S McIlhaney Jr. and McKissic Bush in *Hooked: New Science on How Casual Sex is Affect-ing Our Children* (Northfield Publishing, Chicago, IL, 2008) on page 41

15 Ibid.

16 Rob Bell's *Sex God: Exploring the Endless Connections between Sexuality and Spirituality* (Grand Rapids, MI: Zondervan, 2007) again. Page 139

17 The article was for New Zealand but talked about the global average, as of 2007. (http://www.smh.com.au/articles/2007/10/13/1191696214489.html)

18 Thats from a Centers for Disease Control 2002 study. (http://www.cdc.gov/nchs/data/series/sr_23/sr23_024FactSheet.pdf)

19 Thanks Shaun Alexander and Cecil Murphey for *Touchdown Alexander: My Story of Faith, Football, and Pursuing the Dream* (Eugene, OR: Harvest House Publishers, 2006/2007) page 146.

20 I give Kevin Roose some props for this book. It was hilarious and intelligent. And I'm not sure I'd go spend a semester at Liberty like he did. *The Unlikely Disciple: A Sinner's Semester at America's Holiest University* (New York, NY: Grand Central Publishing, 2009) page 228.

nine.

1 Kent McDonald said this. He is a friend and a mentor. He's also very cool.

2 Jonah Lehrer again in *How We Decide* (New York, NY: Houghton Miffin Co., 2009) page 179.

3 Ibid. page 175.

4 Thanks for the honesty Mary Eberstadt in writing: *The Loser Letters: A Comic Tale of Life, Death, and Atheism* (San Francisco, CA: Ignatius Press, 2010) page 8

5 If you're a U2 fan, you should read Steve Stockman's *Walk On: The Spiritual Journey of U2* (Orlando, FL: Relevant Media Group, 2005) The quote is from page 17.

6 Screwtape Proposes a Toast was written later, after the book, and added in later publications. It was worth adding, in my opinion, for that quote alone. Thank you C.S. Lewis: *The Screwtape Letters* (New York, NY: Harper Collins, 1942, 1966) page 189.

ten.

1 Seth Godin again. *Linchpin: Are You Indispensable?* (New York, NY: Portfolio, 2010) pages 110-111

2 Chip Heath and Dan Heath in their book *Switch: How to Change Things When Change is Hard* (New York, NY: Broadway Books, 2010) page 98 use a great analogy of an Elephant and a Rider for the different parts of the brain. Both have their strengths and weaknesses including the fact that the Rider is willing to sacrifice short-term for long term payoffs and the Elephant likes immediate gratification.

3 Ibid.

4 "The Heat of the Moment" is an absolutely stunning study to look through. (http://www.predictablyirrational.com/pdfs/Heat_of_Moment.pdf)

5 Jonah Lehrer on his excellent blog. (http://scienceblogs.com/cortex/2010/02/sex_ed.php)

6 Not a direct quote but communicated in Steve Santagi's *The Manual: A True Bad Boy Explains How Men Think, Date, and Mate – and What Women Can Do to Come Out on Top* (New York, NY: Crown, 2007) and Bradley Gerstman, Christopher Pizzo, and Rich Seldes' *What Men Want* (New York, NY: HarperCollins, 2000).

7 Frederick Buechner writes this one in *Wishful Thinking: A Seeker's ABC* (San Francisco: Harper, 1993) on page 65.

8 Another xxxchurch.com podcast. "Episode Number 2 'Luke'" August 13, 2007

9 My good friend Josh White introduced me to G. K. Chesterton. Thanks Josh. *Orthodoxy* (New York, NY: DoubleDay, 2001) page 55

10 Robert B. Cialdini *Influence: The Psychology of Persuasion* (New York, NY: William Morrow and Company, 1993) page 12.

11 Ibid.

12 Steve Santagi the self-proclaimed "bad boy" again: *The Manual: A True Bad Boy Explains How Men Think, Date, and Mate--and What Women Can Do to Come Out on Top* (New York, NY: Crown Publishing, 2007)

13 Proverbs 5: 3,4

14 Proverbs 7

15 I first heard Gerry Sittser from Whitworth University use this quote at a camp. I later emailed him to send me the quote because I couldn't get it out of my head.

16 A look at the experiment from Philip G. Zimbardo "Stanford Prison Experiment: A Simulation Study of the Psychology of Imprisonment Conducted at Stanford University." (http://www.prisonexp.org/).

17 Malcolm Gladwell is the maestro of looking at things differently and then writing about it. So good. *The Tipping Point: How Little Things Can Make a Big Difference* (New York, NY:Little Brown and Company, 2007) page 160

18 Ibid. page 167

19 Laura Sneade wrote "Date Rape: College's Dirty Secret." in June 2009. Not pretty. (http://oncampus.richmond.edu/academics/journalism/magazine/4-97/features/articles/

gratitude

f-daterape.html)

20 Malcolm Gladwell again: *The Tipping Point: How Little Things Can Make a Big Difference* (New York, NY:Little Brown and Company, 2007) page 163

21 From Genesis 39 – another classic Bible story, about Joseph and Potiphar's wife.

22 Sarah Kliff "Looking for Mr. Clean (and Single)" for Newsweek.com Sep 5 2007 (http://www.newsweek.com/id/42676)

23 Jane Weaver for MSNBC (http://www.msnbc.msn.com/id/17951664)

eleven.

1 Chris Napolitano wrote an article for the New York Times and the Freakanomics guys (another great book and blog) interviewed him. (http://freakonomics.blogs.nytimes.com/2007/08/27/chris-napolitano-on-george-bush-the-state-of-porn-and-why-playboy-doesnt-suck/)

2 Proverbs 31:10, 30.

3 Proverbs 31: 13-19

twelve.

1 "U.S. Divorce Rates for Various Faith Groups, Age Groups and Geographic Areas." Religious-tolerance.org. Updated 6 January 2008.(http://www.religioustolerance.org/chr_dira.htm)

2 "Suicide." Centers for Disease Control. 2008. http://www.cdc.gov/ViolencePrevention/pdf/Suicide-DataSheet-a.pdf.

3 That Poll again. (http://www.washingtonpost.com/wp-dyn/content/article/2007/08/20/AR2007082000451.html)

4 There are lots of marriage books. This is just one chapter. It's simple and general. But maybe it will trigger something in your head to make you want to dig deeper or look further into this mysterious thing called marriage.

5 G.K. Chesterton *The Defendant* (Accessible Publishing Systems, 2008) pages 19-20.

6 C.S. Lewis *Mere Christianity* (HarperCollins: New York, NY, 1952, 1980) page 106

7 Barry Schwartz tell us why we're so stupid in the West. We're trapped with this consumerist mentality and it's killing us. *The Paradox of Choice: Why More is Less* (HarperCollins, New York, NY, 2004) page 106

8 Ibid.

9 1 Timothy 6:10

10 Read Shane Claiborne's *The Irresistible Revolution: Living as an Ordinary Radical* (Grand Rapids, MI: Zondervan, 2006) and you'll be blown away. Great book. A guy who lives what he believes.

11 I've quoted this one already. But it's worth quoting Jane Weaver's "Many Cheat for a Thrill, More Stay True for Love." on MSNBC again. (http://www.msnbc.msn.com/id/17951664)

12 Yes, Rob Bell again. *Sex God: Exploring the Endless Connections between Sexuality and Spirituality* (Grand Rapids, MI: Zondervan, 2007) page 135

13 A great article. Lauren Slater, "Love, The Chemical Reaction," National Geographic February 2006: pg 48.

14 Walter O. Bockting, M.D. and Eli Coleman, PhD obviously have studied this much more than I have. But still I don't think I agree with *Masturbation as Means of Achieving Sexual Health* (Binghamton, NY: The Haworth Press, Inc., 2002) page 7.

thirteen.

1 C.S. Lewis *Mere Christianity* (New York, NY, Harper Collins, 2001) page 156

2 Hosea 3:1.

3 Hosea 11:8-9.

4 John chapter 14.

5 Matthew 3, Matthew 12, and Matthew 23 are all examples, but there are plenty of harsh words throughout the Bible to the religious – those who think they have it all figured out.

6 Matthew chapter 7 verses 15 to 20

7 When I read that line in Huston Smith's *The Soul of Christianity* (New York, NY, Harper Collins, 2006) on page 51 I underlined it, marked the page, and immediately typed it up. My copy is filled with underlines.

8 "Born again" has been a little tainted but it's how Jesus seemed to describe this transforming process too in John chapter 3.

fourteen.

1 It seems obvious but if you're married, or in a committed relationship, and have some wounds, constantly bringing them up in front of your spouse is not a way to heal them. Let them go. Let them heal. And dwell in what you have now. If talking about that past girlfriend or boyfriend does not bring beauty, joy, delight, precious, or good to your current relationship, why say it?

2 Philippians 4:7.

3 Some classic Tucker Max again on the back of *I Hope They Serve Beer in Hell* (New York, NY: Citadel Press Books, 2006, 2008)

4 Malcolm Gladwell for a final time. This is basically one of the main points of the book but he summarizes it a bit toward the end of *The Tipping Point: How Little Things Can Make a Big Difference* (New York, NY:Little Brown and Company, 2007) page 255-257.

5 Remember when your mom used to say, "If everyone were jumping off of a building, would you jump with them?" Well, even though you would roll your eyes at her, we're all jumping off the building for some reason. So, whether it's being an early adopter as Gladwell calls it, a change leader as the Heath brothers call it, a Linchpin as Godin calls it, or something else... someone, at some point, has to decide to stop jumping off the building. You?

author

Ryan made video games for 12 years, working for the company Cyan. After that he became a pastor. Video games and pastoring have very little to do with each other except they both involve writing and creativity, something Ryan likes very much. Ryan has a wife and three children and lives in Spokane, Washington.

www.thenakedfruit.com

CPSIA information can be obtained
at www.ICGtesting.com
Printed in the USA
BVHW040334310721
612910BV00009B/810